PEACEFUL FREEMAN

A STORY BY A PEACEFUL
FREEMAN ON THE LAND

MICHAEL SINCLAIR-THOMSON

authorHOUSE®

AuthorHouse™ UK
1663 Liberty Drive
Bloomington, IN 47403 USA
www.authorhouse.co.uk
Phone: 0800.197.4150

Published by AuthorHouse 03/06/2018

ISBN: 978-1-5462-8950-0 (sc)
ISBN: 978-1-5462-8951-7 (hc)
ISBN: 978-1-5462-8976-0 (e)

The two most important days in your life are the day
you are born and the day you find out why.
—Mark Twain

This book will contain information about myself, my past, and present. Also there will be four chapters, detailing why I made a life-changing decision to better not just myself, but also my life and much more.

I am a father and a humanitarian. I have degrees in financial advice, photography, and counselling. I am an autodidact, a first responder, and an analytical researcher. I have also studied law and how the control system of the world is when seeing it for what it really is and not just the illusion. I'm an adventurer with a passion for travelling and experiencing different cultures. I'm also a philosopher.

I'm a spiritual man with an enlightened consciousness........
and this is my story.

I am a Welshman who currently resides in The Gambia, West Africa— the smallest country on the 2nd largest continent.

Whilst writing this book, which I have been toying with for a while, an unfortunate incident set me back. I'd actually started a month prior to this writing (December 2014) but my MacBook was stolen with my manuscript stored on it. I was three-quarters of the way through it, and the loss has really pissed me off, as I'm sure you can imagine. So I've decided as of now (1 Jan 2015) I shall start again. Now I have a MacBook Air.

The thief opened my bedroom window whilst I was sleeping, lent in through the bars, and stole my MacBook, my iphone, and my jeans (with my wallet in the pocket). The cheek of it!

So now I have decided to get straight back into this manuscript. As I'm going, I'm trying to recall how it was originally composed. I flick back and forth between the chapters and the introduction, trying to compose it similarly. But it's not working out that way. Still, I'm hoping it will work out well and that all who read — will be able to comprehend it. Please be kind, as *Peaceful Freeman* is my first piece of writing. In addition, I normally find it quite difficult to talk about myself. So I'm out of my comfort zone. Nevertheless, I'm happy to be doing it, as it can only benefit myself in the long run.

I would really like for *Peaceful Freeman* to be interesting and informative as well. I hope it enables readers to become happier, help raise their consciousness, and help realise the true power you have in this world. We are not just homogenous drones. We are real and alive. Our minds are that powerful in this universe. We create our own reality.

Believe in yourself. You must first love yourself, and then others can love you.

Life is great, and it can be for everyone. We just need to believe it can be the way you want it to be. You control your life. Don't allow anyone else to do so, because it's yours, not theirs.

It took me a long time to work this out, but I feel blessed that I have. Some never comprehend this esoteric information, which is terrible.

Belinda Carlisle sings, "Heaven is a Place on Earth." And she is right. For the few who truly believe this earth is heaven, it can be. You can either believe it's hell or heaven. You decide. It's your life.

That is why I'm forever trying to be positive in all aspects of my life. Note that I said "trying". I know that life can be hard sometimes. Thus, "forever trying" is the correct phrase. After all, we are humans with human flaws and feelings—good, bad, mad, sad, angry, happy, joyful, and so on. Let's enjoy all the feelings that we have and learn from our mistakes. If we don't learn, they won't be mistakes; they will be choices.

CONTENTS

CHAPTER 1

A Little about Me and My Life

I was a young naive boy growing up, always trying to please others. I would put myself out to help others. Don't get me wrong; I still do. But there is a limit now, as takers don't have boundaries, which requires givers to put up boundaries. That way, we won't be taken for a ride, as happened to me many times years ago. Now my boundaries allow me only to help those who deserve the help and not just takers taking advantage of my good nature.

I'm pleased I have a good nature. I feel it makes me more of gentlemen than I might otherwise be, and it's nice to be nice. It's nice to be important, but it's more important to be nice.

I wouldn't change any of the experiences I had while growing, as my belief system allows me to comprehend that I would not be who or where I am today without those experiences. And I'm quite content with who I am these days. I wouldn't want it any other way.

I'm living in The Gambia, West Africa, and possibly the happiest I have ever been. I'm nowhere near as naive as I was as a youngster and definitely more confident than I was, as you will find out later in the book.

I truly went from being geeky, naive, nervous, immature, and unintelligent to becoming quite the opposite.

I fortunately realised that my consciousness and intelligence levels were rising and that *I* created my reality and strived to do what I wanted, regardless of how society wanted me to live. So I did. I'm happy to help others realise their potential in life. With a positive mental attitude, you can accomplish the most unbelievable feats—feats you may have at first thought impossible. You can accomplish the types of feats that many courageous, fascinating people do. It's not just them that can do so. We are all human and all capable of greatness, much more than society would have you believe.

This world is topsy-turvy. To make great sense of this asylum we call earth, you will first need to understand how the most insane are running it. (More of that later in *Peaceful Freeman*.)

At around the age of thirteen, I got suspended from school. It wasn't that I was a bad boy. If anything, I was indoctrinated in to the schooling way—don't question anything and do as you're told. But one day, my friend and I did something that was quite unlike us. We held a fellow pupil out of the second-storey window by his legs. I'm not sure what happened for us to have done this. I do remember, though, that it was in our English classroom. Neither of us was a bully, so consequently we both got suspended for two weeks. Looking back now, it was a foolish thing to do; we could have killed the boy. If I remember rightly, we were bunking off assembly. So yes maybe I was a little rebellious in some ways, which would make perfect sense given my rebellious side to date. More will unfold of my rebellious side later on.

Now at my age, I can be truly happy about myself because I'm comfortable with just being me. I know who I am and what I choose to be in this life. I choose to be a happy, with humanity and travelling close to my heart. Doing both is a pure blessing.

I find that so many people choose the material life over a spiritual one. That is down to so many not even trying to see the difference. They are adamant, as they are blinkered to society's way of life.

If all people decided to do a random act of kindness, with an altruistic heart, just once in their life, they would realise the great feeling of oxytocin flowing and enhancing the feeling of greatness and joy that comes from doing something that is inherent in us—something that we are born to do time and time again.

Given the magnificent feeling that overwhelms you as a result of altruism, it's really a selfish way of being selfless.

These acts don't even have to be over-the-top, unheard-of kindnesses. Simply helping a homeless person with some change to help them eat or buy a cup of tea will make a massive difference. Most people are so asleep (subconscious) when they are outside their home, working, travelling, walking, and so forth, that they just don't see what is right in front of them.

The stigma of homeless people is taken somewhat out of term by society. People without homes are frowned upon because brainwashed citizens believe they made themselves homeless and enjoy living that way. *Are you insane?*

Maybe a handful of people a cross the globe do make such a choice. But for the majority, because of society, they have been forced to become homeless either due to rental rates being pushed astronomically high or some other situation. Some quit their jobs to help aged or disabled family members who then, unfortunately, die, leaving the helper subsequently without a job or money to pay rent and so, out, homeless.

I don't just help the homeless because I have been homeless twice. Once I was fortunate to have my car—a mark 3 Toyota Celica—to sleep in. It wasn't the most spacious, but I had heat when needed and a little security garnered through locked doors. Everyone needs a base, somewhere to relax and feel comfortable in safety.

I got back on my feet by securing a security job that gave me a caravan to live in whilst I worked on site.

That was the second time. The first time I had no car, so mainly I was sofa surfing, staying with friends. I felt I was imposing, so having nowhere to go, sometimes I would try and sleep on the bench in the foyer of the local police station. That was nearly impossible because of the shape of the seats. Plus, the police would ask me to leave, even though there was no one else around, as it would be early hours of the morning. They were just being assholes, as I wasn't hurting anyone. I just wanted a dry and secure shelter for the evening.

I fortunately sorted myself out by making a new girlfriend, who just happened to want me to live with her. Within a fortnight, I was employed again. I achieved a position with a sales company that offered a great salary, good commission, and a company car. Life was looking up again.

If you have never been homeless, you can't imagine how detrimental it is, in terms of emotional/mental and physical well-being. No one should be homeless, and no one should starve. The queen of England is so demonic. With the wealth she has and is still acquiring, she wouldn't even miss the amount it would take to eradicate poverty and starvation across the globe.

Even the amount of money it takes to go to war far surpasses the amount it would take to eradicate homelessness and starvation around the world. The greedy oligarchy is too interested in making profit and enslaving us even more.

I have also realised that the more I learn, the more ignorant I feel.

Lets just say knowledge is a tree that I'm climbing, every branch has something new to learn, the tree just keeps growing, with every branch I conquer, numerous more grow.

CHAPTER 2

Why I Decided to Live in a Motorhome

Over the last few years, I owned my own taxi business in Pontypridd, South Wales, United Kingdom. I had a beautiful home in a converted stagecoach house on the land of a stately manor. Located in a town called Penycoedcae, the home had fantastic views and very nice neighbours. There were ten apartments in total, and the owners lived in the manor house. Don, the owner, was a fantastic guy and great friend. His untimely death was a great shock, even though his health had been deteriorating. His loving wife and sons were devastated. Even my neighbours were deeply saddened, as we were all like family. The relationship between neighbours was great. We would all help each other where possible, which is humanity at its best.

After driving my taxi for many years and having a great time, I was earning well and taking many holidays. I was having the materialistic time of my life. Life was great. My friends were awesome.

Then came a turning point in my happiness and life. It all started because I had sex with a crazy woman who claimed I had raped her. Pending her claims, I couldn't drive my taxi for three months until police had cleared me from the investigations due to her lying. In addition, at that time, a few people disliked me, as they thought I had done what the woman was accusing me of. My good name had been tarnished. I didn't even know the girl. I had met her when chatting to my friend. We were all taxi drivers, but she worked a different area.

Whilst all this was going on, I heard she had made these types of allegations before many times. She was clearly seeking attention.

After the police dropped the case, I started taxiing again, and life nearly went back to normal—apart from some sly looks and back-chatting.

Later, when I tried to renew my badge, the taxi licensing agency did not approve the renewal, classing me "not fit and proper." This led me to take action via court proceedings, which was a total waste of time; the court institutions and council agencies all stick together.

Whilst my taxi was being rented out, I had plenty of time to study and take courses. This went on for about a year. I spent a lot of time cycling and doing charity work. I also spent one Christmas helping feed the homeless. But when I arrived with a few others to do the same, we actually got fed ourselves and received presents and watched a film. We took the remainder of the food to a local homeless shelter.

A year passed, so I decided to apply for a new taxi badge. The application was again declined. So I hatched a plan of action. I would study law and take taxi licensing to court.

As time went by, I started to learn more than I'd first anticipated. My consciousness grew leaps and bounds. I started from the start—common law—and then worked my way towards maritime admiralty law, which is the inception of statute law. I came to realise all statute laws were a money-making scam for the government and, of course, their bosses, the bankers.

This was when my eyes started to open—when I started to comprehend how the real world is run and not just see the world the way the oligarchy want us to see it. Finding this esoteric information very interesting, I decided to dig deeper—so deep that, with all the research I did, I have come to the conclusion that we are chattel to the hierarchy. We are mere slaves to debt.

We are in a perpetual state of subconsciousness. Technically, the majority don't even wake to drive or work or play sports. We have been brainwashed into thinking materialism is how we should live, and the nine-to-five workday is the bare minimum we should put in. We need to work extremely long hours so we can buy shit we don't need. That way, by acquiring a bunch of stuff, we can look as though we are doing better than others. Plus my car and house need to be bigger than yours to make me feel more of a man.

What a crock of shit that is. Well done, Satan, for making us think we're not special in every single way imaginable. We are all spiritual beings with the gift of living. A lot of people believe life is about is going to school to get a qualification to get a job to work ridiculous hours to pay the bills, get married and have kids, work, work, work; watch mindless TV; pay taxes; grow old; and die.

Life is much broader than that. So in *Peaceful Freeman*, I shall explain how I broke free from the mental slavery and how, to date, billions of people remain imprisoned by their own thoughts and beliefs about the world.

The oligarchy owns the mainstream media, Hollywood, sports, the music industry, governments, the majority of famous people, the banks, MKUltra, suppressed technology—everything needed to keep the rest of us dumbed down and subconscious. Those with power want you to be homogenous drones. Stay asleep. Do not question authority. Consume. Money is your god.

Please watch the 1988 movie *They Live* with Roddy Piper to really get to grips with how 99 per cent of the population is being controlled subliminally.

This really gets me down that this is going on. As John Lennon, said, "Our society is run by insane people for insane objectives. I think we're being run by maniacs for maniacal ends, and I think I'm liable to be put away as insane for expressing that. That's what's insane about it." The people who make all the decisions comprise 1 per cent of the world population—the thirty-third degree Freemasons who run around Bohemian Grove naked, as well as performing sacrificial ceremonies.

These guys are batshit crazy. They're all about secret societies and backhanded handshakes.

The Satan spawn that these guys are will use all sorts of ways to keep us submissive and maintain the status quo, including Sigils, movies, Disney cartoons and movies, TV shows, and news, all containing subliminal messages and a lot of lies. There are six corporations that run 99 per cent of the world news, so it's easy to ensure propaganda. Walt Disney was a thirty-third-degree Freemason. The thirty-third degree is the highest degree in Scottish rite Freemasonry, as thirty-three is the number of years old Jesus Christ was when he was crucified. But the Freemasons don't honour Jesus or God the divine creator. They honour Lucifer. This is why the world is in such a mess—filled with wars, killing, and negative news. Free power is hidden from the masses, along with cures for all diseases. We have debt currency through the Rothschild dynasty, as well as a fractional banking system. The love of money is the root of all evil.

We have so many homeless people and so many people who are starving worldwide because the 1 per cent want more for themselves and less for us. This is despicable, and it's only going to get worse if we sit back and do nothing. I do like to see there are protests going on across the globe. We need to stick up for our rights, as they are slowly being eroded through arbitrary statutes that the majority of people believe are *laws*. So people pay the fines they receive, as they think they are breaking a law.

All you are doing if no one has complained about you is breaking a rule set up to keep us enslaved. We are debt slaves.

A settlement certificate, also known as a "Birth Certificate" since 1837, is an official document issued to validly recorded poor (paupers) granting them certain basic rights and entitlement to benefits in exchange for recognition of their status as being owned as "property" and lawful slaves.

https://escapeesblog.wordpress.com/2012/01/09/birth-settlement-certificates/

The number of people who have been placed in jail due to these arbitrary statutes is unbelievable. This is especially true of trials in maritime admiralty courts. Such courts are not common law courts but, rather, for-profit courts, just like prisons are run for profit. The same is true for police stations, social services, and all courts other than courts de jure (Latin for "in law"). The United States of America has opened more prisons than schools, hospitals, or universities because there is big money to be made in prisons. Plus, prisons are cheap worker factories. Sweden is closing prisons as the number of inmates plummet. It's all down to treating them like humans and not just chattel.

Iceland imprisoned bankers so has no Rothschild debt currency. The same is also true in Hungary, North Korea, and other parts of the world where there are no Rothschild debt notes.

Most wars are started because where they're being waged, the Rothschild dynasty doesn't have central banks—Iraq, Afghanistan, Syria, you name it. There is money to be made in stealing the resources of a country and then controlling those resources through debt after the conflict has settled. Clever evil geniuses. The illuminati are satanic despots.

I am writing this book to get this off my chest and hopefully awaken more people to the demonic world we really live in.

The greater the number of people who awaken spiritually, the better the chance we can break free from the mental shackles and live freely, with better education and without indoctrination. Free the suppressed esoteric information on cures for diseases and hidden technology that could improve the lives of billions. This ranges from free power for all through the ionosphere which Nikola Tesla tapped in to the clandestine information that was used by the Egyptians and other pyramid engineers of the Aeon age.

The reason knowledge of these and many more subjects has been suppressed is that there is no money in free power. As is, the big oil corporations and big pharmaceutical companies make trillions of dollars a year. So you being healthy is not a part of their agenda. You being unhealthy—that's what they like. This is why the food industry is rigged so you not only get hooked on food-like products (the stuff you get at fast food restaurants) we also become obese and dependent on the chemically induced, genetically modified crap of the world in our diet.

The governments aren't there for the people. They're there for the bankers and for their own egotistical means.

"Govern" means *control*, and "ment" is old Latin for *mind*. So you get "control - mind" or *mind control*.

Let's similarly break down "mortgage". "Mort" means *death*, and "gage" is simply *gauge*. So we have *death gauge*.

Legalese is the language of statute law. It's just used to bamboozle the laymen into getting legally robbed of our hard-earned money and to take away our God-given inalienable rights.

See *Black's Law Dictionary*. "Understand"—when police officers or judges ask if you understand, they're not asking if you comprehend as they switch from English to legalese. What they're really asking is, do you stand under our authority.

So it's a trap to get you to agree orally, to bind you to a verbal contract. The way the hierarchy work is by contracts, either written or verbal.

Please see *Black's Law Dictionary* for an understanding of the terms "artificial person" and "natural person." An artificial person is your straw man—in other words, your birth certificate, driving license, passport, utility bills, parking fines, taxes, and so on, anything with your name in *capital letters*. This is called *Capitis Dominutia Maxima* your legal fiction. Yes, that's right, legal fiction, meaning maximum loss of status. (See settlement Certificate, as stated earlier in the book)

Your corporation name, the natural person, where you're the natural person—a man or a woman living and breathing and made up of skin, blood and bones etcetera.

This is why, whenever you register anything, you pass over ownership. Do you think you can own anything under this corrupt satanic system? That is a most definite *no*.

You pass over ownership of your children, your car, anything you register. That is why you are only the *registered keeper* and not the owner of your car. The reason this is done is to further the control system.

"Legal/lawful"—let's get this straight. These words have two meanings (yes two, not one). "Legal" is applied to something that is given the force of law with consent of the governed. So in summary, if you say yes when police officers or judges ask if you understand ("stand under" their authority), then you have agreed to a verbal contract.

If you say, "I comprehend what you're saying, but I don't understand, then you haven't given them any power over you. That is why I claim common law every time.

"Common law" means *no harm or loss*. That covers all eventualities. If no one has complained about you, no law has been broken.

"Statute law" refers to anyway the legal mafia (government) can take money from you. This includes things like seat belt, parking, and speeding fines; taxes; fees for licenses and passports; and so on.

A "summons" is an invitation. So, as with any invitation, it can be declined. However, many people think a summons is something that has to be accepted. *Wrong*.

To "summon" is something only witches and wizards can do.

All these words come from aeons past.

Fear factor is how the illusion works. What people think is, if they don't go to court, the situation will be worse for them.

I happen to accept my summons, as I know my capabilities in court. I have personally, on three occasions, peacefully made the magistrates run out of the court. This happened once in Cardiff magistrates, and twice in Pontypridd magistrates court, also in South Wales, United Kingdom. I accomplished this by turning up with my birth certificate,(Settlement Certificate) not giving jurisdiction, and knowing exactly what to say and when to say it. This is especially true when I'm asking judges for their attestation/oath of office; this works, as most magistrates and judges work for maritime admiralty courts, (Not court de jure courts) —from magistrates to the high court in London— are run-for-profit courts. Dun and bradstreet, http://www.dnb.com enables you to see if companies are worth doing business with and up to how much in currency pounds sterling for the United Kingdom. (Also note that police stations, social services, political parties,

As many judges don't have an oath of office, this is called "malfeasance" in a public office and illegal. So when you ask to see the oath of office (just like you should ask police officers for their warrant cards) magistrates and judges, more often than not lacking one, get very jumpy. They know you know how the game is played. Under the Magna Carta article 61, the layman (sovereign of the court) has a lawful right to seize the court. That's when they get worried and make a sharp exit. So then, as I'm the sovereign in the court, I declare the case closed without ill will, vexation, frivolity and, of course, without prejudice; thank the court; and walk away, a free man.

If everyone realised they could do the same, then people would have more of their hard-earned money in their pockets and less fear.

As you can read, I'm very disappointed with the way in which the world is being run by maniacs who are only out for themselves. My belief system allows me to believe that, if you're egotistical, then you are comprehending only the human experience. If you are being or becoming spiritual, then you comprehend that we are souls/spiritual beings living a human experience for a small amount of time in our whole intergalactic and beyond experiences.

CHAPTER 3

My Love of Travelling

My love of travelling first started when I went to Spain as a child with my mother and brother. It was the first time my brother and I had been on a plane and travelled. I always used to think that Spain was far away and that the planet was huge. But then as you travel more extensively over the years, you come to the conclusion that it's not really that big. After all, if you can fly somewhere in a few hours, you can drive the same distance in a few days.

Flying to many countries, not just as a holiday but also to live, broadens your horizons, gives you more confidence, empowers you, and also gives you a real feel for that country.

You learn the following points about a place:

Culture, especially in Australia
Currency
Values
History
Local languages
Local bylaws
Borders
Police
Military
Corruption, in Senegal
Serenity
Peace, in The Gambia
Cities

Beaches, in Miami
Countryside
Presidents
Prime ministers
Dictators
Political protests, especially in Venice
Churches
Mosques
Leisure centres, especially in Austria
Hamams (Turkish baths), especially in Morocco
Weather
Itineraries
Flights
Ferries
Wars
Architecture, especially in Prague
Bars
Restaurants, especially in Budapest, Hungary, Buda side
of the river
Bicycles, especially in Holland
Cars, especially in Cuba
Technology
Local cuisine
Kibbutz, in Israel
And much, much more

There is nothing better than experiencing all of these aspects of different places and more. You can never get a better feel of the sights and smells of a country in any way other than experiencing it for yourself. Not even travel documentaries are quite as revelatory, as they share the presenter's thoughts and feelings about a particular country. You will always have your own experience, as we don't see with our eyes, we don't feel with our hands, and we don't smell with our noses. Likewise, we don't taste with our mouths. All of these body parts are just sensors for our brains to interpret through chemicals. The images our eyes "see" are simply mental projections of the physical world around us.

Our consciousness of the world is very important—much more important than being highly educated. Many highly educated people are extremely dull in other areas and possibly only indoctrinated in the field in which they acquired their education.

Education doesn't prove intelligence, just as age doesn't prove maturity.

This is where a lot of people get confused. It's very sad but very true. This is why I thank God for providing me with intelligence and the ability to be an autodidact. I use critical thinking with a trivium thought process. I also decalcified my pineal gland, which is also called the third eye (This refers to the gate that leads to the inner realms and space of higher consciousness). Thus helps with a higher comprehension of my spiritual being, also my belief system about the world around me, including my wakefulness.

The only person you should try and better is the person you were yesterday.

Wisdom is better than silver or gold.

Emancipate yourself from mental slavery, none but ourselves can free our minds.

Happiness is not a station you arrive at, but a manner of travelling.

There is only one person who could ever make you happy, and that person is you.

Our minds are products of our brains.

Everyone wants to tell you what to do and what's good for you. They don't want you to find your own answers. They want you to believe theirs.

There are no ordinary moments; there is always something going on.

This moment is the only thing that matters.

Sometimes you have to lose your mind before you can come to your senses.

A peaceful warrior acts. Only a fool reacts

The most difficult thing in life is to know yourself.

Who looks outside, Dreams, Who looks inside, Awakes

He who conquers others is strong. He who conquers himself is mighty.

Life moves pretty fast. If you don't stop and look around once in a while, you could miss it.

Life is short. Break the rules. Forgive quickly. Kiss slowly. Love truly. Laugh uncontrollably. And never regret anything that made you smile.

I'm always thinking of where to travel to next. My plan was to be in Thailand after the sale of my motorhome in The Gambia, West Africa, but God has a specific plan for all of us. So I shall incorporate his plan into my paradigm and visit Asia at a later date and carry on working and living in The Gambia for now. I'll put off travelling for a short time—until I start putting my big plan of visiting even more countries into action. Such plans include driving across the United States of America, South America, and Canada in a motorhome. I'm not a stranger to achieving a long road trip, which will be explained in my next chapter, A narrative of a drive spanning twenty-three countries, two continents, four ferries, and one desert, achieved in 2014.

CHAPTER 4

One Absolutely Amazing Road Trip

The year 2014 was an amazing year for me. And, I'm sure, my good friend Jamal Rapscallion Baig would say the same thing. Together, we travelled to some amazingly breathtaking countries on a road trip that was decided after many months of planning.

I decided to go for a very extensive drive and offered for my long-time friend Jamal to come along. I did make the same offer to a few other friends as well, among them Jason Bad Boi Brazier and Gavin Rips Jones. But, unlike Jamal, they all had families and commitments.

"The Beast"

So Jamal decided that, as a fellow lover of travelling, he would set out with me a few months later for an epic road trip across Eurasia to see his brother in Thailand. Such a journey was well and truly possible and not out of the realms of my driving skills. So for a while that was the plan, until it changed. Jamal kept working to fund this epic journey.

I was working in Coventry, England, at the time after having sold my taxi business. To stop myself from getting bored and also to raise some more funds for the *big* off. After booking a holiday to Portugal just before Christmas 2013, I received a phone call from an old friend Jamie Gwynne, asking if I would team up with him working for the water board. He'd been offered a job working with the board. As the position I held with my job wasn't benefiting me much, I accepted. I said I would start the day after I returned from Portugal.

After a nice relaxing week away in Albufeira, Portugal (and no arguments or food that had been thrown by Helen Champion this time), we arrived back in the United Kingdom. We drove from East Midlands Airport, England, to Coventry to drop Helen off and then straight down to Barry in South Wales, UK, where I parked my motorhome on Jamie's drive, ready to be inducted in work the next day.

The induction went well, and we started working very hard and long hours and making good money. At first, we were told this was a permanent position so the travelling would go on the back-burner for a while longer. In that time, I kitted out the motorhome with another leisure battery for long periods of stay. I also purchased two 12-volt HD televisions for "The Beast" (my new nickname for the motorhome}. Christmas and New Year's went by with many hours spent at work and a New Year's Eve party.

We were doing our work before time and making good names for ourselves for works done well. Then the water board hit us with a bombshell. We were getting laid off. We were blown away, as we had been promised it was a full-time position. But that was cool. We even worked the weekend after getting laid off, but our manager really wanted to keep us. But last ones in, first ones out unfortunately.

We were told on the Wednesday we were getting laid off Friday, so I mentioned to Jamal that we would be leaving very soon. We both agreed we would leave on 6 March 2014, which was fine, as that gave me plenty of time to sort out my odds and ends so I could travel with no return date.

Most friends said we would probably only spend two weeks in Holland and then return. Little did they know, when I go travelling, I don't do things by half. We had rearranged the end destination, having decided to see more of Europe first. So our plan was not set in stone. We did know that, at the very least, we were going to visit Amsterdam Holland, Prague, Czech Republic, Hungary, and Slovenia. As it would turn out, that was just the start. We drove an explored 20 countries. I then went on to experience twenty-three countries, two continents, four ferries, and one desert. And I am still here in The Gambia, West Africa, having arrived just shy of six months.

So whilst we said goodbye to all the night of the sixth, we headed to Cardiff first to pick up one last important gadget before we sailed the next morning, all keen, happy, and eager to go. After the purchase was complete, Jamal informed me that he'd left his sleeping bag and all his bedding back at his house. So after I had gone red in the face for a second, I said, "No worries. Let's go get your things." It wasn't the greatest of starts. But for a friend and to save his pocket we drove back the twelve-ish miles through bumper-to-bumper traffic at the heart of rush hour to get his things. Then we loaded up again, and for the second time, we were off, waving goodbye to his family.

Now we were really off. The Beast was filled with smiles, laughter, and happiness as we imagined all we were going to experience. We truly had no idea it could be as good as it would turn out. But we were ready for it. So with singing and a bit of dancing, we drove out of Wales through England to the Harwich ferry Port, where we parked by the security booths, ready for the 8:00 a.m. ferry. We got in the back. Jamal started to manoeuvre the sofa into his bed, whilst I dived in to my *huge* comfortable bed and then slept until the morning.

Bang. Bang. Bang.

I arouse to loud banging coming from the door. It was a polite wake-up call from the passport control officers saying, "It's time to board the ferry."

We got up, changed, and drove through passport control. Then after a short wait, we were permitted to board. At this time our excitement was showing on our faces. We were offskies.

I passed the long ferry journey going from watching the sea to a movie and reading. After what seemed like a long time of anticipation, we could see land. *Boom.* There was Holland. We packed all our things and went down to the Beast.

We disembarked the ferry, and I drove us to the Dam (Amsterdam), Holland. Along the way, we continued laughing and joking and enjoying the sites, the windmills, and the beautiful architecture of Holland.

Once we arrived, we filled the tank up with diesel. We'd made it from Wales on one full tank. Very happy with that, we asked directions to somewhere quiet we could park for the night. Speaking in broken English, the attendant at the petrol station gave us some shoddy directions somewhere. We headed in the direction he mentioned and just happened to find an amazing place to park for the evening. We found a great restaurant and then enjoyed a nice cold lager and some food. The waitress was made more attractive to me because she was so intelligent. (I'm also sapiosexual).

On that note we left there to find a shop selling cannabis for a little recreational and, of course, medicinal use.

That evening after we returned to the Beast, the toilet cartridge was emptied into a drain, and we smoked some local goodness and laughed till we slept.

The next morning, we awoke to a market right outside the Beast. Being well happy with this, we had a look around and then chowed down on a lovely breakfast in a restaurant opposite the Beast.

We then got ourselves together and walked to the ferry to take us across to the city. We realised we were wearing winter clothes when the sun came out and it became a beautiful day. After walking around for a while, I treated myself to a Thai massage, which was well deserved. When it started to get dark, we decided we would go and eat at the restaurant near the Beast. We had our food with a few lagers and then enjoyed a smoke back at the Beast—another night finished with laughter.

We awoke to another beautiful day in the Dam, got dressed accordingly, and went out for breakfast. After a considerably long breakfast, we headed back to the Beast to assemble the bikes and cycle around the Dam. As we were assembling the bikes in the glorious weather, we could hear sly remarks next to us over the smell from the shit cartridge we'd dumped two nights before over the drain. It was stinking.

Whoops. We laughed quite hard and made a quick getaway on the bikes.

We cycled off and joined the ferry. This was clearly the only way to get around the Dam. We cycled for a few hours and took some amazing photos. I had one near scrape with a tram, so my ass was twitching at that point for a short time.

Then it was decided to lock the bikes up and find nice restaurant for lunch. We walked around and found the Bulldog (a restaurant and bar). I was very happy as the establishment was playing a rugby game on the TV. So we ordered food, ate, and then moved to a better position for the match. We started some rugby banter up with the English supporters who were there. And what started out as just a random encounter with Hana Smith turned into a fantastic day and night. Hana sat and chatted with us whilst we were watching the game, as she was also from Wales but working in the Dam. She was also there supporting Wales in the rugby game.

Hana mentioned she was going to meet her friend Sarah Blakemore and asked if we would still be there when she returned in around five to ten minutes.

We said, "Yes."

Hana left, and we went back to the banter with the English supporters, enjoying the game and having a few drinks, happy times.

Hana re-emerged with Sarah Blakemore, another beautiful woman, so we were very happy when they asked if they could join us. We, of course, like gentlemen said, "That's fine."

It wasn't long after that we were getting on quite well and someone mentioned tequilas. That may have been me. So a few rounds of tequilas came out, and we were on it and having a blast with two beautiful and intelligent women. We lost in the rugby that time. But it wasn't the end of the world, as we had great company.

We left the Bulldog, as Hana wanted to show us a real local bar. Grabbing the bikes, we headed over for a few more lagers and laughs, which we certainly had.

Many tequilas later, we decided to call it a night and part ways. Very drunk, we cuddled and thanked each other for a very enjoyable evening. I won't mention the sneaky kiss I had from Hana.

We grabbed our bikes from outside and cycled back to the ferry and then onward to the Beast. After a little smoke, we slept, planning to hit Germany the next day.

After a long drive to Germany, we decided on going to Berlin to see the historic wall, which was a great decision. The only downside was the spot where we parked ended up being a bit shady. What had seemed from a distance a normal park setting—kids playing, walkers, families having picnics, dog walkers about, and so on and so forth—had a sinister side underneath. At first look, everything seemed fine. But eerily, at both ends of the park was a group of Rastafarians selling cannabis. That in itself would not be a problem if there was just one offering, as he would just be acting in commerce. But the group made me nervous, and each end reminded me of the Steven Seagal movie called *Marked for Death*. It seemed very ominous at the time. After we passed there, everything was fine.

The Berlin Wall was a sight to see. Even though the wall was a lot shorter now, it was still a marvel to see with artwork painted on it.

In the souvenir shop located between the two remaining walls, we had photographs taken with a tommy gun and authentic headwear from that era. After taking a multitude of pictures in the shop and around the wall, we left, only for me to return to have my passport stamped with authentic stamps of the day. So the unfortunate walk through the ominous park happened a few times more than originally planned. But it was worth it—until I had my passport stolen in The Gambia (more on that later).

Later that evening, a nice meal and few German lagers went down very nicely, whilst Jamal enjoyed a nice glass of tea. Then we slept in preparation for nothing big day's drive.

The next day, we drove to Poland. This road trip was now starting to take shape. We were heading into unchartered territory, which was great. And the further we travelled, the more exited we were becoming. We didn't stay long in Poland—just a drive through, one stop for an evening meal, and then sleep. The next day we were ready for Prague, Czech Republic, for a few days.

I had been to Prague before, but Jamal hadn't. So I showed him around. We cycled the first day, as we had arrived early enough.

The first stop on the bikes was Tesco for soft drinks and chewing gum. We also stopped to get local currency—attaining cash back after paying for items with my bank card. Then we were set. We rode around Prague, an absolutely stunning city with amazing architecture. A distinguishing feature is that the city has no bullet holes, as do many other countries in

Europe. The Germans took Prague as a base, so the city suffered no bullet damage. The opposite is true of Dunkirk in France, which seems to have more bullet holes showing than the walls themselves.

Jamal and I were making friends and cycling around Prague.

This city was where I first test rode a Segway. These machines are awesome. At first, I was a bit weary so had a shaky start. But very soon, I came to relax and enjoy the simplicity of this incredibly powerful transportation tool, thanks to one of the pub crawl representatives.

We then moved on, and Jamal made a new friend. Gold Dust was a mime artist dressed all in gold, and this was only to be the first of many on our travels. So subsequently, a quick picture was taken, and off we went.

Later that day, after placing the bikes back in the motorhome, we dressed for a night out and left for a tantalising meal. Next, we had a few drinks in what I call "the cave bar" near Charles Bridge. There we had an eye-pleasing sample of the local strippers who stripped on the bar. It was very entertaining. Jamal made another friend, Gold Dust 2 (a man in what was a gold gimp suit as he didn't even have a mouth hole to drink through). After laughing at his clubbing outfit, we actually had a laugh with him.

We left there after a few drinks at about 1.00 a.m. and headed not just for any old nightclub. We went to the second largest nightclub in Western Europe. It is huge; fair play, it has nine large areas playing different types of music. One is in the cellar, and then each of the four floors above features two huge nightclubs separated by stairs. We were partial to two of the nine clubs and spent most of the time in those. But we did circulate to enjoy the company of others in the other sections as well.

Around 4.00 a.m., it was time to leave and head back to the Beast for a sleep.

At approximately 4.30am and still dark under the dim light of the street lamps, we arrived at the Beast. I then noticed damage to my side window. I was now confronted with a crime scene, the side window, including the blind, was broken. I realised I had to open the door to see if anyone was inside or discover whether anything had been stolen. I unlocked the door and opened it. I looked in, and to my amazement I found …nothing had been disturbed. I went from total disappointment to realising it wasn't that bad after all, considering. It was just vandalism that could be and was semi-repaired in a very short time.

On brainstorming the options in this position, I rolled the ripped blind out of the way, with masking tape, I temporarily fixed the plastic window back into place so we could sleep and then call the police to report the crime in the morning. After repairing the damage to a high standard, we got our heads down for a few hours so we could deal with the day ahead.

Later that morning we awoke to another sunny day. After breakfast was made and consumed, we were ready to involve the police and get a crime reference number for my insurance.

We then, after waiting a few minutes, spotted a police car slowing to the traffic lights next to us. We called for the officer to pull over, and they did. After they got out of the police car, I explained the best I could, as the language barrier was present once again. With pointing and many hand signals, they got the idea and radioed for an English-speaking colleague to help us in this matter. I was very impressed with the service and pleasantness of the policemen and women that were helping us.

A short while later, the English-speaking policeman turned up and was very honest and polite, which was very refreshing. He admitted there probably wasn't anyway of finding the vandal(s), as there were no cameras covering the area. I knew as much anyway so wasn't concerned with that.

He said, "After 2.00 p.m., please come to the police station for your crime reference report."

We thanked the officers after getting directions to the station, and off they went.

At that point, lunch was in order. So after we frequented a local eatery for a couple of cheeseburgers and chips, we made our way to the police station. With little bother, we found it. We waited a few minutes and then spoke to a policeman, who subsequently went off and reappeared with the said document. With that, we thanked him for their help and left.

Upon returning to the Beast, we decided to park in a different location. We didn't make the decision solely for safety reasons. We also didn't want to pay for parking. So we drove around the corner and parked outside a restaurant, hoping to use the establishment's Wi-Fi from inside the Beast also.

After locating what seemed to be the restaurants Wi-Fi signal, we went in to acquire the password and have a water.

After getting the Wi-Fi code and chatting, we were getting on well with the staff and showed them our drive so far on Google maps. They were amazed we had come so far. Then I showed them our plan was eventually to make it to Africa. What I could see in their eyes and micro-expressions told me they thought I wasn't serious or couldn't do it. But they were very nice and accommodating anyway. They explained it was a paid parking area outside and the traffic wardens were around frequently. Not being concerned with tickets—it's the clamps that worry me—we brainstormed and decided to push on. We thanked the staff and departed.

That evening, we arrived in Austria. As it was late, I spotted a large hard shoulder and pulled over for the night, only leaving us a few miles from Vienna, which would be our next day's new city to explore and enjoy.

Boom—the seventh country in seven days.

Fortunately, Austria was one of the countries where we could use our mobile phones as if we were home, as we were both on the same mobile network. After catching up with friends from back home using the 3 (3 is the mobile phone company name) network, we were very happy. Plus, the speed of the Internet was really quick. We could stream music from Internet stations at home, which was nice. We listened till we slept in preparation for the next day's full day of exploring another country.

The next morning after breakfast, we headed into the Big Smoke. (Big smoke is my nickname for Big cities). In Vienna, the first plan was to park the Beast and have a walk around to see what Vienna had to offer. From the safe-looking place we found to park, we could see a leisure centre. After the last few days of washing with wet wipes to get the grime off and not using the on-board shower, we knew it was time to visit this leisure centre for a shave, a shower, and to enjoy the facilities.

So with a quick kit bag assortment of fresh clothes and toiletries, I was ready. Jamal sorted his, and we headed on in.

Once in, we realised how expensive the centre was to use. However, as we still had euros with us, we paid regardless and went in. After having a good shave, I headed on upstairs to the sauna and pool area. As I entered the area, I was told by a patron, speaking broken English, that no shorts were allowed. Noting that the few others there were only wearing towels,

I headed back downstairs to the changing room to leave my shorts in the locker and headed back up wearing just a towel.

On passing Jamal, who was still shaving, I mentioned to him the protocol. He looked a bit bemused. We bantered for a minute, and then I headed up once again. When I first entered the steam room, no one was around. I lay down to relax. A minute later, Jamal stepped in and relaxed on the next wooden bench over. We went on conversing, only wearing a towel and no shorts, which was very unusual to us.

Another patron walked in and relaxed over the other side. After a minute of silence he spoke in German, thinking we were locals.

We both replied, "We don't speak German."

"Arrrrrgggghhhhh," he said in his German accent. "English?"

"No. Welsh," we said, as the Welsh do.

I then looked over to see who I was speaking to. As quick as I did so, I looked at Jamal, who was, by then, looking directly at me with what I can only describe as a look of, *What on earth!?*

He must have had the same thought I had. At that point, we discovered why the Austrians don't wear shorts or bathing outfits. They lie naked on their towels. After our initial shock, the man explained to us to that we should undo our tightly wrapped towels and be open and free. At first, I could see Jamal was as uncomfortable as I was about doing this. Straight away, a very attractive woman walked in. As a world traveller, I waited to see if this lady would do the same, only in the interest of understanding the cultural ways of Austria. She eloquently disrobed, laid the towel on the wooden bench, and glided to a lying down position—all in a move I perceived to be one fell swoop. There she was, lying down completely naked. I felt out of sorts. I then removed my towel from the front of my body so as to match with the locals. At first this seemed out of my comfort zone. After a short while and seeing many others do the same in certain areas of the health suite, however, I felt a lot more relaxed and had come to terms with the nudity, it feeling very natural and freeing.

After a few hours of relaxing and taking it easy, a feeling of hunger came over me. Jamal is no stranger to eating, so it was decided we would leave and find some good food in Vienna.

Vienna was so windy that day, for the first time, I needed a fleece. Inbound we went. When we crossed one of the bridges to head in, we first started to admire the architecture, most importantly one of the cathedrals. It was exquisite, not just in size but also in the detail of the statues and how it was crafted over time to create a perfectly shaped cathedral. We walked inside, and it was even more impressive. I cannot put into words the impressiveness of every single detail of every statue and wall plaque. The stained-glass windows enhanced the majesty of this breathtakingly beautiful, righteously dated place. I was amazed by the sight and texture. That is definitely an understatement of how truly amazing the cathedral was.

After experiencing what humankind had done centuries ago, we came across a protest—a demonstration of what humankind can do today, fighting for freedom in a peaceful way. A group of Syrians was protesting for their fellows.

I am personally impressed when people stand up for what is right in this world. Everyone deserves to live in peace.

After making friends and taking pictures we moved on impatiently, hunting for a moderately priced lunch.

Jamal and I protesting

After walking around for what seemed like an eternity, we decided to split up and eat. I headed into a Japanese restaurant, which was a first for me. I picked something that sounded nice from the menu. To my surprise, not only did I enjoy it, my mouth was filled with flavour. My taste buds were having a tantalising time with every chew and every mouthful. I didn't want the food I was eating to finish, but unfortunately all good things come to an end.

I was at that time toying with the idea of gluttony when I spotted Jamal through the window. He was passing by, so I called him. He told me he had eaten just a few doors away. Then I explained how much of fan I had become of Japanese food and that I would definitely be consuming more in the future. I still haven't to date, but I will even if I have to fly to Japan, which would also give me a chance to experience their culture.

We left the restaurant to head back to the Beast. Fortunately we did at that time, as a tow truck had arrived to tow the Beast away.

So with a quick leap to the driver's seat, we vacated the scene. With almost lightning speed reflexes, we were on the main highway heading out of Austria. By then, we had realised we needed to pay to use the roads from service station tills in incremented days or months. With that, we were on our way out of the country. I thought better of it and hit the gas. We were out of there!

Next stop, Slovakia, though only for a quick drive through and a stop in Bratislava for a few pictures outside the presidential palace. We saw the changing of the guards—more egotistical crap—and we were off again.

Next up was Budapest, Hungary. This city was quite special. We spent nearly a week here, as it was quite nice, with plenty of Turkish baths and a great city to cycle around, as well as superb weather. We found a little place that was perfect for our needs.

The food was fantastic. One Thai restaurant blew my mind with its seafood dish.

Buda, as well as the other part of the river, Pest, is beautiful in every way, especially the top of the mountain with the views and statues.

The only downside to Budapest was that the Beast was broken into one evening. We came back from chatting with some great girls in the local health suite, and I discovered that the door to the Beast was unlocked. Knowing that wasn't a good sign, as I always lock the Beast by regimental standards, I opened the door to see what I could see. At first look, nothing major was different from the snapshot I always subconsciously take in my head when closing the door and locking up, apart from cables on the floor. On closer inspection, I noticed my iPad was missing with a little currency inside my iPad case. Jamal, on closer inspection, had his hair clippers stolen. So being truly gutted that someone had been in the Beast without permission and stolen from us, I quickly started to think of the positives. The doors and locks were still in great condition, as the thieves had picked the lock and only stolen material things from Jamal and I. At first, Jamal was gutted. Then he started to not worry so much, as he had another pair of hair clippers anyway, even though they had stolen his better ones.

So that night it was decided to wait until the morning to involve the police for yet another crime reference number/report for my insurance.

On a solemn note, it was time to call it a night.

After breakfast, it was time to get hold of the police. I walked over to a very small café next to where we had parked and tried my best to explain to the locals I needed the police. "Could you please help me?" I said.

After twenty minutes of hand gestures to all at the café, one older gentleman caught the gist of what I was saying and called the police for me. I thanked them all for their assistance and for their patience with my plea.

On returning to the Beast, the police turned up forthwith and, in their broken English, asked if we would follow in the Beast to the police station. Naturally, we followed to get the process underway. When we arrived at the police station, I parked outside where one policeman checked the locks were working on the Beast and then led us inside. After we'd waited five minutes, a bilingual woman hired by the police turned up to take our statements. She took Jamal's first. I was then asked by a policeman to go outside again to check whether or not the Beast's door locks were secure. Out we went. He tried all the handles and was content that all the locks were working effectively. We then returned to the police station. He relayed the details in Hungarian to the woman and then promptly went away.

Jamal gave her his statement of events, and then so did I. She then told us to come back later for the crime reference report.

As it's fresh in my mind, I have to tell a part of the story Jamal might not like me mentioning. But, hey ho, it made us both laugh uncontrollably many, many times over the trip. Sorry, Jamal, rudest baig. But it's a *must*!

I have to mention that, at sporadic times on this trip, it wasn't just Jamal who spend a long, long, long time in the toilet. I did too mostly. As

I like to say, I'm inventing. It's just ludicrously funny. You would have to be there on all these occasions to grasp how intensely funny it was.

I shall try and explain why.

I'm sure you can possibly imagine, whilst being in a restaurant, your friend leaves the table to go to the toilet. "No worries," I hear you say. "Happens all the time." But this is where the difference comes in. Your friend would probably take a maximum of say five minutes. My friend can take up to an hour. So here is what happens when your friend leaves for such a preposterous amount of time. Firstly the waiter or waitress or, in some cases both, start looking over after fifteen minutes have gone by thinking, *Has his friend done a runner without paying?* All the while, you know he hasn't. Then the looks get even more concerned after twenty minutes have gone by, whilst I am starting to chuckle, thinking, *How can one man spend so long in a little cubicle?*

Then you start clocking the waiters/waitresses watching you. I really start to belly laugh after thirty minutes. Some patrons would haven eaten, drank, and left well before this time, so they are even more concerned over the time you are spending just sitting chuckling to yourself. By now, they must be thinking he's definitely left the restaurant, so are just hoping I pay for his also.

After forty-five minutes go by, they are now possibly wondering if I am just sitting there as I can't afford to pay and worried about what will transpire with no way of paying. They start wondering if I'm going to try an escape without paying. All this is what I'm concluding by the way their eyes and micro-expressions are when they look over at the table at me. All is well, as I know Jamal will be back. I don't know when the funniest part is. As soon as I see him returning, I start laughing, even more because I know he's just been to use the toilet like anyone else, only for an age longer. Jamal also used to do the same when I would come out of the toilet, but I would never stay in as long as him.

So as we were leaving the restaurant three hours after having arrived— that's when we would both use the toilet, one right after each other. We'd spend nearly an hour each just in the cubicle in the toilets. This didn't happen every time thankfully, but sometimes it did.

Even if the waiter/waitress knew he was in the toilet, it would still make me laugh. Also my mind would make me think that they were thinking something dodgy was going on or about to happen. That thought would make me laugh even more. I would imagine the waiter/waitress thinking he might be doing drugs in there. I knew Jamal definitely wasn't into that, so it was even funnier for me thinking that.

This went on throughout the trip. I could hear Jamal laughing before I had even left the toilet at places where the table was close to the toilet entrance. That, in turn—even if wasn't hearing but just knew he was laughing—would make me belly laugh. Then I'd stay in there even longer, laughing and trying to stop laughing before I left, which never worked. Other toilet users might have been thinking, *Who is this* crazy *in the cubicle laughing?*

As a side note, I laughed throughout writing that passage, as it was just that funny, even recalling those times. Sorry, Jamal, but it was a *must*! You well remember how funny it was. Even our good friend, Matjaz Vidali, will remember this happening when we were in Slovenia. (More on Matjaz, as well as Slovenia, later in the book.)

After a long, long lunch because of Jamal's toilet break, we went back to the police station in Buda. Yes, Buda, this side of the river. After waiting for a short time for the crime reference report, what I can only describe as a very loud man with a very deep voice entered the building. At first we couldn't see the man who entered, as the front doors to the building were around the corner and down a few steps.

At first I looked at Jamal, and he looked at me with the same expression—one that asked, *What on earth like?* (In Welsh, "like" is an unneeded add-on to any phrase but is added because we are Welsh.)

As the deep-voiced loud man was speaking in Hungarian, we had no idea what he was saying. At first I thought he might have worked there and was the big boss reprimanding his staff for some reason. After a minute or two had passed, I could hear this booming-voiced man getting closer. Just then, he emerged. Coming around the corner, he at first seemed to be The Incredible Hulk, and he was heading towards the waiting area where we were. With another quick look and a snigger towards Jamal's direction, I noticed my expression was mirrored by Jamal's. We were looking back at this strange Goliath of a man mountain walking towards where we were sitting and continuing to speak like someone was listening to him from two streets away—in Hungarian. I still had no idea what his gripe was about, but I started laughing straight away, as he seemed crazy. Fair play to Jamal restraining himself from belly laughing out loud. There was no way I could stop.

The man stopped walking at this point and looked at me, whilst still moaning in Hungarian. I continued to laugh, as it was too hard to stop. He then, looking very smart even in his green overcoat, sat down on a chair. I then started to smell alcohol coming from the Hulk. I continued to laugh, as I couldn't believe my eyes or ears and what had just arrived. He tried to speak to us in his broken English but soon went back to griping over something or another in hungarian. So laughing again was inevitable. Jamal still trying to suppress his chuckles but didn't succeed this time.

We later found out that he was there complaining that someone had stolen his phone, which was only fair. But then the police mentioned, "He's been coming here for many weeks."

So without any more evidence the police could do no more for him. He left, still moaning loudly as could be.

Then a policeman came over and gave me the crime reference report. We left. As it was so late, we drove back to the same car park, knowing we could park there. Plus we knew we weren't leaving the Beast. We knew it would be fine for the evening and then decided to move on in the morning.

The next morning after breakfast, we went looking for water to fill the on-board bowsers. After driving around for ten minutes, we passed a fire station. With a quick U-turn, we parked in the car park. I headed to the front door to speak with the staff. After five Hungarians tried to communicate with me, at least one spoke English and agreed they would fill up my bowsers. I was asked to drive around the back.

Driving in through the gates, we were amazed to see antique fire engines. Immediately after parking by the hose, we asked why they were there. They promptly explained and showed us these dated, well-maintained fire engines. They even explained they had been decommissioned only a few years earlier. We were blown away to learn that they were still being used after the '70s, let alone until 2012. So a few pictures were in order. We explained how far we had come and where we were heading. They were very impressed. With that, we said, "Thank you and goodbye." Then we left and were off to another country.

Next up, Croatia—the only border in mainland Europe that we could see was still in place to check passports. Even though Croatia is in the European Union, they still had checkpoints just like Gibraltar. Subsequently, after a quick search of the Beast, we were through. Once over a bridge, we could see how primitive Croatia was. Spotting a Lidl's, we stopped for snacks and drinks. Trying to work out the Croatian currency, we at first worked it out to be cheap. But when at the till, I only bought nuts as they cost the equivalent of £6, I put the rest of the shopping back and only got robbed for the nuts.

Leaving there, we headed for the capitol, Zagreb. We spun the Beast around and headed west. A few hundred yards up the road, what did we come across? A police checkpoint. As we were the only ones on the road, the officers flagged us to stop. I pulled in to the lay-by, stopped, and said, "Hello. How are you guys"?

They replied, "Very good. How are you? And where are you from?" As they could possibly tell from number plate and steering wheel position, we were a long way from home. We spoke to them for a while. Jamal was talking football. After they looked at my documents, they mentioned I didn't have my lights on. I mentioned it was the middle of the day, and there was an abundance of light. They explained that their policy is to enforce laws (legalities) of Croatia, and that meant for a good few months of the year, you need to drive with your lights on twenty-four hours a day. I did explain there was plenty of daylight, and as they'd asked so nicely I switched the lights on when I left. Then I turned them off later, as it was ridiculous to keep them on in the middle of the day. At that point, we realised why everyone had been flashing us in Poland.

Later we arrived in Zagreb. After driving through the city, we looked for a quiet safe place to park for the evening. And we found one, right next to a great-looking church with a big car park.

After parking nicely, it was wash, change clothes, and out for dinner. We walked to the local pub. No food there, so went to the restaurant across the road. Too late. Food finished—even though it wasn't that late. So back in the Beast we went. We drove to town and asked locals there for a nice place for food and Wi-Fi. We got directions for a pizzeria two blocks down. So we went for a stroll down the road. After turning the corner, we found a pizzeria.

As we walked in, one polite waiter said, "I'm sorry. We have a private party. Please follow me. I'll show you another pizzeria."

We walked three doors down. As we entered the other pizzeria, the waiter from the other restaurant came in and started speaking with the other waiter. They both then served us politely and made us feel at home by seating us and serving us drinks and menus.

We logged into the Wi-Fi and chilled with some Croatia radio playing some great tunes. After the first waiter said his goodbyes and left, our waiter went out the back to make us the pizza's we'd ordered. I then found out that the music we were listening to was an Internet radio station, which I made my default radio station for a long time.

After a great pizza (and I'm not a massive pizza lover), we went back to find the church car park to park for the evening.

The next day, we arose to the sound of a church choir singing, which was pretty awesome—good songs and great voices. As I looked out, I was gobsmacked. There were nearly a hundred cars surrounding us. There had been only us parked there in the evening, and we hadn't even heard one car enter the car park, let alone the twenty that were parked in the very near vicinity. That day, we felt so comfortable. We chilled and relaxed there, only to go out later in the evening for a beverage and Wi-Fi. At that point, we decided the next day, we were going to see my mate, Matjaz, Mat for short, in Slovenia.

The next day, it rained heavily, so I contacted Matjaz via Facebook and said we were on route to Slovenia. Matjaz and I had met in Miami a few years before and had stayed in touch. We learned about each other's awakening to the real world since we'd last met.

He had mentioned earlier that I should come visit him when I was passing, so I said I would. Just as we were about to set off, he messaged, saying, "That's great. Here's my number phone for when you're getting closer."

Onward and upward we headed for Slovenia. We passed through Croatia's border crossing once again and were in Slovenia. The first town we came to we looked for a phone. After hunting for Wi-Fi for twenty minutes with no luck, I asked a woman working in a restaurant if she could phone my friend's number for me. The fine lady wasn't an English speaker, so with hand gestures, I got the message over. I spoke with Mat, and he gave me directions to his home town, Kranj.

"Okay," I said. "I'll call when we're there."

I thanked the lady for the use of the phone and asked directions out of town, and away we went.

As the capitol, Ljubljana, was on the way, we passed through to have a flying visit and take some pictures. We stopped just long enough for Jamal to buy a tuna sandwich, and then on to Kranj we went.

On route to Kranj, we were privileged to see one of the most spectacular sights in the world. Right in front of us were the Alps, looking high and mighty and glowing in majestic abundance for all to see, with snow-capped peaks to the ridged solid even-chiselled face.

We made our way to Kranj. The first stop was the train station. At first, it looked like it had been closed down. It was so quiet, apart from a few lonely-looking cars in the car park.

From where I was parked, I could see what looked like a café. *Closed*, I thought. I headed on over just to see. I pushed the door, expecting it to be locked shut. To my amazement, it was open. I entered and at first thought I was walking in to a very dark 1970's post office. But on further inspection, I could see it was a very small café. I asked if the place had a phone. The lady behind the counter said in her broken English, "Sorry. No phone." But she did offer the use of her mobile. She phoned Mat and explained that I was at the café.

His reply was, "I will be right there."

Ten minutes past, and Mat was there, large as life, a big smile on his face. I too had a big smile, as it was a pleasure to see him again. We had become good friends in Miami. A big man hug ensued. I introduced him to Jamal, and they hugged too.

Mat offered for us to have a drink in the café. We accepted, expecting to have a coffee or even push the boat out and have a beer. But mat had other ideas. So he ordered from the waitress—three tequilas or something just as potent.

I was shocked. I didn't even know the café did spirits. As they were being poured, we were discussing our time in Miami, Florida, where we visited the world's largest yacht/boat exhibition. It was absolutely out of this world. I wouldn't have gone if Mat hadn't mentioned it at the hostel where we'd met and where we were both staying. We became friends and went to the exhibition together. Mat is a captain. He is qualified to circumnavigate the globe. That is why he wanted to go. I also like boats and yachts so was keen to go and see some mind-blowing yachts and even all the gadgets and gizmos that go with them. The exhibition also had a separate hall filled with fishing equipment to fit on your yachts and boats and the like. In one large shop area, there were two full-blown fishing seats—the type that sit at the back of yachts where the professionals fish from. They were set up for a fishing battle, both chairs facing each other, so the owner tempted us to win T-shirts with a fish battle. Mat and I were in. We took to our chairs and made ready to let the battle commence. The two shop workers harnessed us in to the chairs and gave us some tips. Then it was *on*.

I had never fished in my life, so Mat had the biggest advantage. The two rods were connected by a line, and there was a red cloth attached in the middle. Whoever got the red cloth closer to them passing a certain mark first won.

Now it was battle time. With a three …two …one countdown, it was on. Battling with the rod, I'm trying to reel in what feels like a whale. I'm winding the reel in as frantically as possible and then letting the rod go and then reeling in and pulling the rod back. This went on for a few minutes. The shop workers were calling for us to pull. They were getting as excited as us. "Come on," they were saying, giving me tips at the same time, as I wasn't even sure of what I was doing.

Then the buzzer sounded. That was it. Battle over. Not even sure what had just happened, I was unharnessed. I stepped down, wondering who'd won and whether I was even doing it right. I walked over to Mat. The shop owner passed us both T-shirts, saying well done to us both. I deciphered that Mat had won. I shook his hand, saying, "Well done, Mat." I was well pleased with my free T-shirt. Even though I didn't win, it was worth the battle anyway, as it was loads of fun. I felt it in my muscles afterwards.

I explained all this to Jamal at the café while we were swigging back tequila and lagers.

We also found out more of each other's awakening and how our respective awakenings had affected our lives. We were both amazed at how much our outlook and careers had changed because of this skyrocketing conscious shift. Even Jamal, as intelligent as he is, was amazed that we, Mat and I, had done our research so well. All our answers about world events coincided.

That week, our stay in Slovenia was great. Mat is a great friend, host, and tour guide. We were even invited to stay in his man cave whilst we were there and ate and drank with his father and friends. We tried Balkan food, which was very meaty and very tasty. Morning, noon, and night in Slovenia is a good time to have tequila or some very strong alcoholic shot. Even by my standard, shots for breakfast is normally unheard of. But, as they say, when in Rome …

Mat's friends are awesome. We enjoyed spending hours conversing in the local bar at night, swapping ideas, thoughts, truths, and beliefs.

After spending almost a week with Mat, his father, and his friends, Jamal and I decided to move on to the next country. So after the big thank you and goodbyes also a little repair to the television aerial on the Beast that had come loose, we were on route once again.

Next country would be—*boom*—Italy, for the first time for both of us. When we crossed over into Italy, the first port of call would be Venice. So we headed over and arrived very late. We found a great place to park for the night, so we could have a full day in Venice.

That morning, we had breakfast, got the bikes out of the boot, and cycled towards Venice along the highway. For safety sake, I mainly used the pavement; Italian drivers are crazy. I soon realised I was better off on the road due to flying bugs and flies. It was unreal. No wonder nobody walks across the long bridge to the island of Venice. Thus, I was back on to the road; I passed the petrol station and went over the little bridge. After taking a few pictures, we locked the bikes up and decided to walk around.

Just after we'd locked the bikes up and headed in, we were amazed at the sheer beauty that was Venice. It was majestic in all departments—water, boats, gondolas, and architecture. Venice was a sight to behold. After being taken back in ore, we met a very nice Mexican woman called Anna Valiente. We helped her locate a church on the local map she was looking for and then ate some Venetian ice cream together with her, before parting ways.

Jamal and I headed back around, still being taken back by Venice and how breathtaking it was, in culture and architecture.

It was very expensive, though. A short gondola ride cost £60. We walked around the corner into one of the main open areas and stumbled across a protest. After finding out it was for a great cause, we took pictures with banners in hand and danced to the reggae music that was playing. There were so many people holding a peaceful protest, which is great. Most people there had raised consciousness. They were protesting in order to make the world a better place and building awareness for others.

After walking around for a while taking in all the sights and sounds Venice had to offer, we headed back to the bikes and cycled back to the Beast. After grabbing some food in Lidl's supermarket, we headed back to sleep for another day in Venice.

This time, we took the bus in. Being that it was a scorching hot day, naturally, I was wearing shorts and a T-shirt. Everyone else on the long bendy bus was wearing clothes for a winter's day—large heavy coats and jeans. The smell was so bad; way to much sweat smell was in the air. It was buzzing.

Fortunately, we weren't on the bus for long. After spending the morning walking around Venice, we decided to move on. So we caught a bus back to the Beast. We had seen all and wanted to move on.

As we set of with the Beast, we were thinking, *Next stop, Rome.* But that idea soon changed when we were passing Rimini, as Jamal mentioned it was a lovely seaside town that his mother used to visit years ago and that it was a beautiful place. We decided to stay at least for one night. We parked right on the seafront. It was perfect—free parking, beautiful views, restaurants and shops close by.

Subsequently, we had a quick wash and change. Then we headed out for an evening meal and to experience all Rimini has to offer. After spending two days swimming in the sea, shopping, exercising, and eating. Then we moved on to San Marino, another country and, ultimately, one of the smallest countries on earth. It is just a mountain, with one main road elevating to the crescent. Funnily enough, the same road heads down and back out. I'm not sure why it's a separate country, given its smallness. Plus, from a tourist's perspective, it's hardly any different.

So onward an upward; next stop, Rome.

Rome was somewhere we were both keen to visit, mainly because of the Colosseum.

We arrived in Rome to find burnt-out cars that were parked in the street and a very eerie atmosphere. But we progressed on to find a parking spot so that we could head out for food and have a quick look for a charger lead that I required to charge my phone before the shops shut. Time was escaping us.

We parked in a very busy street with plenty of other cars and pedestrians, along with a bus stop right by the side us. After washing and changing for the evening, we flew out for my charger and food. In addition, we were very excited about seeing the Colosseum the next day.

As we headed towards what we thought was the busy part of town, we asked a woman for directions. She was a star. She actually showed us— after a quick pit stop to her apartment for her to drop something off. She explained whilst we walked that she was from an island just of the coast of southern Italy, and she was a student in Rome. After taking us to a place she recommended, a few restaurants and eateries, we thanked her, and off she left. I grabbed myself the charger that was needed from an outside vender, and then food time it was. So we found what seemed to be a great fresh sandwich shop. We entered and chose the fresh sandwich fillings and bread for the woman at the shop to make our sandwiches. In broken English, the two shop staff conversed with us, explaining the history of that area of Rome.

After a very enjoyable sandwich, we started to head back to the Beast. On route, we spotted a bar so stopped to enjoy the local fluids on offer. Very nice indeed. Plus great service also from this little bar.

After an hour or so we left and walked back the half mile to the Beast to sleep for a big day at the Colosseum and Vatican City.

The next day, after waking and eating breakfast, we set off to visit the awe-inspiring Colosseum. Walking towards this magnificent spectacle, I was overwhelmed by its beauty. Even with as much death that occurred there many moons ago, it really is breathtaking. We took pictures of us with the Colosseum in the background and then got into the queue to pay. Then we went straight in to the heart of it, and *wow*.

Words can't explain how incredible it is. What a sight to see. The next few hours were spent taking photos and exploring all areas of the Colosseum and becoming immersed in the history and magnificence of the Colosseum. After that, we headed out to catch a bus to the Vatican. On route, you get to marvel at Rome's spectacular buildings. They have so much history. It is very impressive.

We then travelled on the bus. We were excited to be told to head down that road to the Vatican. We headed on down. And as we crossed the bridge heading to the Vatican, we could see many people hanging around the main road with cameras, along with reporters and cameramen. Seeing one lady standing on the pavement I asked, "What is everyone doing?"

She replied, "The Queen of England is coming to see the Pope."

One minute later, we could see the queen's ostentatious cavalcade cruise towards us. And there she was, the goat-legged lizard, waving to the brainwashed crowd thinking she was something she isn't, on route to do business with another egotistical fraudster who most think is a great man. He's nothing but another paedophilic satanic puppet for the oligarchy.

I don't make wild accusations, so when I say things like above, its not to hurt, its said in truth.

There is so much overwhelming evidence to prove my statements are factual. non-believers just need time to study for this to be proved without quiver-cation.

Here are two web pages to get you started if interested in, pure truth. Just remember all freemasons stick together.

Also don't forget to watch the true movie "Spotlight" starring Mark Ruffalo.

The Queen has a lot to answer for, including the 10 Canadian Kamloops children that went missing never to be seen again, when her and husband Prince Phillip had custody back in September 1964.

https://indianinthemachine.wordpress.com/2011/03/01/the-strange-story-of-the-queen-and-the-children-who-disappeared-from-native-residential-schools/

http://www.collective-evolution.com/2016/08/12/the-vatican-has-paid-close-to-4-billion-to-settle-child-molestation-lawsuits/

You guys don't need me to explain, I know you are all intelligent enough to do your own research.

Nevertheless, the simple fact that I don't like these heartless tools doesn't stop me from going to Vatican City. It also doesn't stop me from being in awe of the architecture and time spent erecting these remarkable buildings.

Vatican City is another very small country. After taking more pictures and enjoying the sunlight—it was an extremely nice day—we headed back. After a short bus ride, we had a little way to go by foot. This time, I had a very bad feeling something had happened to the Beast. I was thinking maybe it had been graffitied or sprayed somehow. But I wasn't too worried even if it was, we would still enjoy the road trip regardless.

Returning to the Beast after putting the key in the side door, I looked inside the window and saw all my clothes in a messy pile on my sofa. I knew this wasn't a good sign. In addition, I realised at that point that the door was unlocked. I knew someone had been in the Beast. I threw the door open and jumped in to see what had happened.

It was a ransacked mess. Thieves had been in and turned everything over. They'd stolen many items and broken the TV above my bed trying to steal that also.

Grrrrrrrrrrrrrrrr! Dirty scumbags. After assessing what had been stolen and damaged, we attempted to communicate with locals to have the police come to yet another crime scene. After a total lack of communication and a waste of time, I left Jamal to look after the Beast whilst I located a police station. After hunting for what seemed like an eternity and dropping in on another station that seemed like a police station but couldn't take my complaint, I eventually found the correct station. Fortunately, there was a bilingual lady who helped me communicate with the police—who were not interested in my dilemma in anyway. One copper asked in a flippant way, "Was it your phone or wallet stolen?" assuming I was an average tourist with no clue.

I explained what had happened.

The police blatantly didn't care and handed me a form to fill in. I filled in the form, and then they pointed for me to go upstairs and wait.

I went upstairs and waited for ten minutes, whilst a plain-clothes copper was dealing with some locals. When he was ready, I entered his office. I explained again what had happened. He filled in his own form and then begrudgingly gave me a copy with a crime reference number, as I wasn't leaving without one.

I returned to the Beast with a pizza to share with Jamal and decided that, since it was so late, we would remain there and leave in the morning.

The next morning we awoke to a sunny day and were pleased to be heading out of Rome and north towards France. After breakfast, we were ready to go.

At this point, we weren't worried about what had been taken and broken. We could carry on the journey. The main downside that Jamal mentioned was his passport. I had told the Italian police about his passport. We could still move on, as he wouldn't need another one until Gibraltar.

Getting into the drivers seat and ready to go, I manoeuvred the car keys to the ignition. After a second or so, I could feel the key wasn't going in to the ignition as freely as it normally did. Upon closer inspection, I noticed the ignition barrel had been damaged. The thieves had tried to steal the Beast. At this point now, I was thinking, *Oh shit.*

After careful consideration, I decided against calling someone and that I would take matters in to my own hands. Through social media, I contacted an old friend who had some experience wrapping ignitions. Whilst waiting for his reply, we started to try and snap the steering lock with our hands and feet, having no joy.

Then I had a reply. It said, "Do not snap steering lock with force, as it can snap the steering wheel off."

So much of a car thief I am. With that information at hand, I started to chisel away at the ignition barrel. This went on for an hour to two.

The crazy thing about this was that many people passing by on foot or in cars could see me smashing my hammer towards the ignition barrel, and not one person said anything. It was like this was something that happened every day in Rome. Crazy eh. The local bus would stop right next to me, letting passengers on and off, and they just looked like there was nothing unusual going on. Even the police drove past once. I expected them to turn around. But noooooo. They must have been on their way to lunch or something.

Two hours went by and I had the ignition in pieces, so I hot-wired the beast. *Boom*, it started—happy times. Jamal looked shocked but delighted we would be off. I then went to drive out off the car parking space and … uh-ohhhhhhhhhh!

Steering lock still on. I pulled back into the spot, thinking, *Are we ever going to leave here?*

After examining the ignition barrel for some time, I noticed very small clips. After I had pushed the clip through the whole, the remainder of the ignition came right out in my hands. I then pushed the steering wheel to see if it turned. Fortunately, it did, to our delight. And thanking God, we left Rome and its thieves. We were glad to have seen what we had seen, and now we were very pleased to leave.

With no ignition barrel and just wrapped wires, we were heading to France with a few stops on the way.

First stop, the Leaning Tower of Pisa, a great place to stop and take pictures. I had only seen it a few times on TV. Jamal mentioned it had been on the movie *Superman* when he'd temporarily become evil and had straightened it. Then later, good Superman returned and pushed it back so it was the leaning tower again.

Next stop, Genoa, a beautiful seaside village. We enjoyed the day and night there and then, in the morning we had to leave hastily.

The reason we had to evacuate Genoa so quickly, in the morning, there was a knock at the door. Two police constables were outside. We answered, wondering what they wanted.

In the worst English I'd ever heard, they mentioned, "Faeces under the Beast."

They asked Jamal to go outside fortunately, as I was belly laughing so hard. (This is not something I would normally find funny, but here it was, for whatever reason.)

I had dumped the toilet cartridge under the beast during the night. So whilst I was laughing hysterically, I could hear the police saying, "Is this your faeces under the vehicle?"

Whilst remaining inside and laughing my bollocks off, I heard Jamal say, "That's not ours. We heard some drunks passing late last night. They must have dumped it there after rocking the motorhome."

Good blag, Jamal, I thought. *Very good.*

Whilst I was still laughing, a second police car turned up. Jamal then jumped back into the Beast. Whilst I was in tears laughing so much, he explained that some woman had phoned the police to complain about the smell.

As they had no evidence or confession, they asked us to leave Genoa. So very quickly, I fastened the motorhome secure to drive away, and with a straight face, I calmly walked around to the driver's door, unlocked it, and stepped in. Jamal had done the same and was sat in the passenger seat ready to go at this point. Normally, it would have been easy to start with a key and drive away. Sixty seconds or less, and we'd be gone. But noooooooooooo! Still with a straight face, I lowered my head away from their eyes. All four coppers were glaring at me. I was behind the dash, as I needed to hot-wire the Beast, wrap insulation tape around the wires, and then position them out of the way, which took a minute or so. As I looked back up, they where still glaring at me. So still with a straight face, which was becoming extremely difficult, I manoeuvred out of the parking place and passed the coppers, who continued glaring as I went. Then my mouth dropped, and all that came out was uncontrollable laughter.

How pathetic was that woman to complain. It was no different from a dog fouling in the road. Plus, two police cars for faeces in the street and not one for an attempt at stealing the beast in Rome. Italian police had their principles all wrong.

From Genoa, Italy, to Montpellier, France, it was all coastline and beaches. *Boom*—such beautiful scenery all the way.

Next stop, France. We blasted to what used to be the old border and then parked just inside France in a town called Menton. What a charmingly beautiful seaside town. We made some great friends there and smoked some French shit. We had parked right by the beach, and it was a stunning part of the French Riviera—one of the most beautiful places I have ever been to. I felt especially blessed whilst swimming in the sea,

Italian Mountains to the one side and the French seaside town Menton to the other—absolutely stunning.

After spending a few fantastic days there, we moved on through Saint Tropez straight along the coast to Monaco, which was a sight to see—huge yachts, perfect tarmac, and some very impressive cars. After driving the track for a short time, as there was nothing left to see, it was a quick fill-up in the tiny but expensive petrol station, and we moved on, coast-bound through the French Riviera, Nice, and Cannes. Not seeing too much there, we pushed on.

The French Riviera truly has some superlative beaches and very friendly French folk. After spending some great days and nights on these beautiful beaches, we left Montpellier and drove inland to Toulouse, only to get stuck in traffic and get bogged down with city life. Having just left the beaches to move into a huge city environment, I personally didn't feel the same. Even Jamal mentioned he wasn't as comfortable in the city as he had been when we were travelling along the beach. A decision was made—let's get out of here. So we did.

The next stop was Andorra. This was a great stop up in the snowy mountains. We enjoyed the food, the locals, and the other tourists. Plus we found a really good gym in the heart of Andorra la Vella, the capital. We did have the beast slightly overheating climbing this huge mountain. But that was the only issue we had with her all trip, and it didn't stop us from reaching the top. Plus I found the reason for the overheating in Morocco (more details to come).

At one of the restaurants there, I tried beef fondue for the first time. And wow, it was very nice. We chowed down on that big time. We had spent a couple of days in Andorra; even though it was freezing cold, it had breathtaking views, great bars, and friendly locals—well, mostly anyway.

One evening, we had the local boy racers turn up as we were trying to sleep. I gave one of the noisiest ones the nickname Wayne, and his chums. Throughout the whole trip, we would give names to people based on their ways or type. That way, we could just say the name, and we would both know exactly what we thought of that person, which was hilarious. Wayne was the boy racer. Tariq would be the blackest man in sight (only because Jamal is brown like his siblings, so it's a running joke between him and his brother Tariq).

Dwayne or the Rock Johnson would be Jamal, as he thought he looked like him. Vin Diesel would be me, as Jamal thought I looked like him. Lance Armstrong would be any cyclist. We used names like Dewi, Dessy, and many others.

I just remembered, in the sauna at the leisure centre in Andorra la Vella, I started laughing. For what reason I was laughing, I can't be sure. But after laughing for only a short time—what seemed to be like a few minutes—the other patrons went from giving me sly looks to belly laughing themselves. It really does happen. It's not just something you see on TV. It really happens. And it wasn't just there. It happened in Budapest. When others laugh, it's very hard for you to stop. But that kind of laughter gives you a great feeling, as your brain releases endorphins that make you feel great.

After Wayne and his chums made too much noise the one night, we left the next day. Heading down the huge mountain away from the snow and back into the glorious warmth, I could smell my brakes. Pheeeewwwwww. The burning smell was coming from the discs, so we stopped at a garage for a short time so they could cool down. We had brunch and were off again.

Next country, Spain—pure warmth. I knew of a great seaside town called Lloret de Mar. We headed towards the beach. On route, we actually missed the right road. So after getting directions from the garage and an ice cream, we could see the sign that said, "France." So yes we did. I drove straight past the sign, turned around, and pulled over. Both doors flew open, and we both jumped out and touched terra firma. With our feet then back in, and then headed in the right direction to Lloret de Mar.

The reason we did this was because we actually stood in three European countries that same morning. Andorra, Spain and France.

We spent just one night at Lloret de Mar. As it was a very well-known destination for the Brits, I had been there a few times before. We went shopping, ate locally, and not much else before we were off again. I'm very sure this was the last place I ate poison from a fast food restaurant called Burger King.

We left because we had become accustomed to relaxing beaches without so many people and tourists. So by cruising down the coast of Spain slowly and staying at the best beaches for swimming and eating, we well and truly found some really beautiful beaches and some great towns and cities along the way.

Barcelona was a great city. We saw a lot of it. Jamal thoroughly enjoyed exploring the local football ground. We met some amazing people. Plus we had a great time watching a very big match in Spain. Real Madrid and Barcelona that night. Even though I'm more of a rugby fan, even I enjoyed that match, as we were in a great pub with an awesome atmosphere. After me sinking back a few class lagers and Jamal enjoying his favourite Tipple cider, we left to try and find the Beast. Much fun was had on the way. I even got away with not paying for any of the busses there, as well as in Rome or Venice. Just lucky I guess.

What was funny is, when waiting for what we were hoping was the right bus at the right stop, I mentioned to Jamal that I was off to find a toilet. I went scouting around for a restaurant or bar with a toilet I could use. Spotting one close by, I left Jamal and the woman I was speaking to and walked into the restaurant. I asked nicely where the toilet was I was told there were no toilet facilities for non-customers.

I said, "You could have helped, but you have given me so much more."

With my nose up in the air and feeling a little disgruntled, I was not going to leave without annoying the jobsworth. As I turned to leave, I spotted my chance. I went out through the double doors and turned. Once I was far enough away but at a place where they could see, I turned, positioned by body so I was facing their restaurant wall and made it look as if I was about to unzip, and let the fluid flow onto the pavement.

With this, I heard what I was waiting for, apart from the girly scream. "What do you think you are doing?" said the waiter as he jogged towards me.

I turned with my hands raised to my shoulders and my trousers zipped, buttoned and belted, I shrugged. "Nothing," I said.

With that I used my swagger and walked back to the bus stop to see Jamal and the bus stop woman just looking my way in a bemused way. I felt great walking away. A real wind up, that's me. But I had been very disappointed about being told I couldn't use the toilet, as it would not have harmed him at all to allow me to use the toilet.

Fortunately, we took the right bus back up the hill for a sleep, as it was very late.

The next morning, we drove off for the next place. As I was searching for the way off this hill and back to the main road, we spotted a water pump at the side of a roundabout. We decided to fill up our empty water bottles, as the water was very good here. This was surprising, as some parts of Spain have very dirty undrinkable water from the taps.

Whilst we were out, we bumped into two very lovely ladies who would become great friends of ours, Wendy Dejesus and Hannah Metvier. We all hit it off straight away. I offered them a lift to the bottom of the hill, where they could get a bus. We had a great chat and swapped Facebook details. These lovely ladies were from America on holiday in Spain. We said we should keep in touch, and that is just what we did. (More on that later in the book.)

We slowly cruised down the coast and stopped at many great beaches on the way to swim, exercise, and just enjoy the great sunshine and, of course, all the local woman who came to the beaches also.

What happened over the next few weeks was incredible. I received a message from an old friend, Anthony Bloom, saying, he and his family were staying at Hotel Playa in Benidorm. "Come and have a drink with us?" he asked.

I replied, "Okay. It might be late by the time we arrive in Benidorm, but will call you when there."

We arrived in Benidorm and located the hotel, where we met up with them and had a few free drinks from the all-inclusive bar. Cheers, Bloom. We had a good catch-up and called it a night.

The next day was great. Jamal and I spent the day in the hotel pool, chatting with the holiday girls, who were supplying us with the free drinks they were getting as they were all-inclusive. Lying in the pool with the sun shining down and having free food and alcohol served to me was the best. That was how it started—two weeks free in Benidorm, living the life of being on holiday on a holiday!

The decision was made to get two wristbands from the girls, who were leaving. That way, we too could enjoy the benefits, which included free food and drink, use of the pools, and on and on in both this and the Hotel Playa's sister hotel, fifty yards away.

This was the start of a great second holiday for us. The first time we walked in to the canteen to chow down on our first of many free meals was hilarious. We were both constantly laughing, as this was a victimless crime.

We felt a little bad but just walked past the staff, feeling confident enough that they would think we are staying in the hotel. Well why wouldn't they? We were wearing the wristbands. With what felt like my balls hanging to the floor as they were so big, I just strolled around, using the pool, getting free drinks from the bar, watching the nightly entertainment, and making some great friends while we were there. We actually got away with it for just over two weeks. Whilst we were there, our good friends we met in Barcelona, Wendy Dejesus and Hannah Metvier, came to see us. Wendy and Hannah are very special to us. They truly are lovely ladies. They came and stayed in the hotel whose facilities we were enjoying.

We got away with our ploy. We of course slept in the motorhome and just used the facilities of the two hotels. Primarily, we used the one up the road, the sister hotel. That's where the canteen was, along with the larger pool and nightly entertainment. Plus, any of the staff who saw us there would think we'd checked into Hotel Playa and just enjoying the facilities of the Hotel Flamingo. We were truly living it up. Plus we had a great night out with the girls—tequilas and beers and super good night. Suck it, slam it, dunk it. That was our motto for the night. *Boom.* Crazy night at Bobby's Bar in Benidorm.

We knew at some point we would have to leave the hotels, but we pushed it as far as we could. One morning after breakfast, I was chilling in the foyer of the hotel using the Wi-Fi when the manager and one of his staff walked past me. The worker pointed me out to the manager. At that point, I knew the game was up.

At that moment, the manager came around behind me and asked, "What room are you staying in?"

My reply was, "I don't answer questions."

He asked another question.

Sticking to my guard I replied once more with, "I don't answer questions."

He then mumbled something under his breath and walked away. I texted Jamal: "We have been rumbled, and I am leaving."

I got up from the seat, walking casually but with haste straight past reception where the manager was standing. I saw the receptionist point to me and say to the manager, "Is that him?" I just heard the manager say, "Yes."

Once I was through the main double doors, I decided not to head towards the motorhome but into town to blend in among the crowd.

I decided to go to Bobby's Bar, as that place has Wi-Fi. That way, I could communicate with Jamal

Five minutes went by, and I received a message from Jamal.

"I'm in Bobby's Bar," I replied.

He replied, "I'll be right there."

Ten minutes later, Jamal turned up.

I asked him, "What happened with you?"

"They stopped me on the way out," he explained. During some discussion, he mentioned he would give them twenty euros. The manager wasn't happy, as he'd asked for fifty euros to try and recover the losses. But he'd accepted twenty euros anyway.

Two weeks all-inclusive for twenty euros—good deal, I say.

Fortunately for me, I didn't give them any money. But we had another issue at hand. Jamal had noticed police at the Beast as he'd left the hotel heading to meet me. So with that, I concocted a plan.

We would leave the bar and head up the side alleys to the Beast. If no one was around, we would jump in and drive, drive, drive straight out of town and head southbound.

Luckily, it was all quiet. So in we got and off we went with arses twitching as we drove out of town, just in case we got spotted by the feds. We hit the highway, and with that, we felt happy we were out of there. Then we started to laugh and recalled the fantastic free two weeks we had just spent there.

We were on our way to Alicante.

Once we arrived in Alicante, we found a great place to park in a very quiet car park with other motorhomes a two-minute walk to the beach. Town was only ten minutes away on foot.

We headed into town for a look around and to have lunch.

We spent the whole weekend in Alicante, as this was the last place on route to get Jamal an emergency passport, as his had been stolen in Rome, Italy, as explained earlier in the book.

Alicante castle was a great tourist attraction. The lift takes you at a very high speed from road level to the top of the mountain where it sits. It was a beautifully sunny day as well.

We even got a ride from the police to locate the British embassy, which had only moved. We literally walked around the whole city back and forth, unable to locate it. Nor did we have any good directions to it. Eventually we found it and were told to come back Monday morning with Jamal's travel plans and cash.

So that weekend we just chilled out in Alicante. Plus we booked the ferry for Morocco. I was looking forward to seeing Gibraltar on route. Unfortunately, Jamal's emergency passport wouldn't allow him to go into Gibraltar and back into Spain, which was where our ferry to Africa was leaving from. The ferries there were half the price of those in Gibraltar, and they came and went more frequently. Jamal also booked his flight home from Marrakesh Airport in Morocco, as he had nearly exhausted all his savings. But that was still a month away.

With receiving his emergency passport and decided to move on southbound. There are some really amazing sights to see. Spain is truly a beautiful country. We stopped at some amazing beaches on route to Gibraltar, including Benalmádena, my brother's favourite holiday destination.

On the way to Gibraltar, Jamal was getting worried he might have to stay in the wild west part of Spain, La Linea, whilst I crossed the border into a British colony. But on the way down, I kept reassuring him that I would smuggle him into the country in plain sight. He wasn't as confident as I was.

At that point, we started seeing the rock (Gibraltar is situated on and around a huge rock) getting closer and closer. We could see the long line of cars waiting to cross the border. Just before it was too late, Jamal said, "Lets do it!" What he meant was, I'm crossing the border with you.

With that said, we were in the queue nudging our way towards passport control. The traffic was moving slowly, slowly—bumper to bumper at this point. Jamal was getting very nervous, but there was no need. If they did spot that his passport didn't entitle him to cross the border, they would have only sent him back—worst-case scenario. But he is a British citizen, so it would have been ludicrous not to allow him into Gibraltar, a British colony.

Now the time had arrived. It was crunch time. I edged ever so to be closer to the Spanish passport control side first. Then I placed Jamal's passport behind mine but showing his picture and details. The Spanish policeman flagged us through. Now we had only one more, and we were in. With a quick flash of the passports through my driver's window, we were waved in by the copper on the Gibraltar side of the border crossing. We were in, Boom; nineteen countries, and this was the first time in history I would become a human trafficker.

Welcome to Gibraltar

Cheeky monkeys at the top of the rock

Making friends in Gib

Gibraltar is a wonderfully enigmatic country. It truly is a magnificent part of the world—from its monkeys to its people and, of course, the huge rock. We spent a long weekend there and made some amazing friends. Thanks Charlotte O'Byrne, Claudine, Lenise, and their friends. They are very aware and awake. And it was an absolute pleasure meeting you girls. You made my stay in Gibraltar a memorable one. Plus I walked across a land border for the first time, with these two lovely ladies, Saphia Mingi and Sarah Smith, we were invited into La Linea, Spain, to meet up with Charlotte for a few drinks and tapas. Jamal stayed in Gib, as he wasn't risking using his emergency passport until we were leaving on Monday for the ferry to Morocco, Mother Africa.

Where we had parked was right at the end by the water, right next to a stunning mosque. It was absolutely stunning when all lit up at night. And from there, on a clear day, you can see Africa. It's totally picturesque.

It's a lovely walk from Spain to the tip of Gib (Gibraltar), especially on a beautiful day. Be very carful driving a tall and long vehicle in Gib, as the roads are very narrow, with tight turns. Also one road is cut into the mountain. It's not very high; I found this out and had to block the road to reverse out.

It's just like Britain when it came to the shops, where you paid in pound sterling. It was the first time we'd used pounds since we'd left the United Kingdom. That worked out well, as I had a stash of coins totalling around fifty pounds. That covered me for the weekend. I didn't have to use my bank card. It's just as expensive there as it is back home. It's much cheaper to go into Spain to eat, drink, and live. But that town "La Linea" is crazy apparently, with the nickname "Wild West".

Monday came and we were keen to hit the big Africa, so we headed out of Gib with no problems. A flash of the passports, and we were back in Spain on route to the ferry. We located the ferry with no problems and parked to the side to sleep before the 8.00 a.m. crossing.

The alarm clock went off in the morning, and we were up, had breakfast. and were ready for the crossing.

Once on board, we had to fill in immigration forms and show passports. That done with no problems, I sat to watch a movie during the very quick crossing. We arrived before the movie finished.

So back to the Beast and drove out of the ferry onto terra firma called Africa. What an amazing continent it is. I'm still here as I write this book and loving the laid-back relaxed feeling and peacefulness.

Me in the big Morocco

Boom. We'd made it to twenty countries.

Once in Morocco, we headed for Tangier's city centre to enjoy some great Moroccan food and experience all Tangier and the rest of Morocco had to offer us. At this point, Jamal still had two weeks left before his flight from Marrakesh Airport.

So on to enjoy we did. Food was very cheap and very tasty We knew Morocco was going to be good to us.

Heading our way slowly down the coast, we were taken back by how different it was from Europe—how life was much freer here, with fewer rules and regulations. The sights, sounds, and smells here were very different but, in all, were splendid.

Casablanca was very similar to European cities in some parts, and as we were not big-city people, we didn't stay there for long and moved on.

The towns between cities can be few and far between but are just amazing. They all have a few shops, markets, barbers, and a teahouse or four.

The barbers here I find are the best in the world. They really make you feel comfortable before they lather your face up, as well as your head. they give you the greatest shave possible, as they do not rush. They do a brilliant job and only charge about twenty dirhams, which isn't even £2.

Morocco is one of the finest countries I have ever been to. The hamams (Turkish baths) are very, very safe.

No one will steal from you in Morocco, because, if people get caught stealing, they will have their hand chopped off. It sounds harsh, but it's a very effective deterrent.

I personally spent six weeks in Morocco, as it's such a beautiful place. I especially enjoyed Imsouane and Paradise Valley, where we met some really great friends of all nationalities, including our good friend Abdou Ryadi and Ayoub. He worked at a little café shack in Imsouane. He made great tea and food. Plus, my first ever surf was there. It's great fun. Most of the world's top surfers surf there, as it has some of the best surf in the world.

Stunning Imsouane

Music night in Imsouane

No animals were harmed; only tin cans got fired at

Making friends and having a laugh on a road trip

Man cave

Imsouane will always hold a place in my heart. It's such a laid-back sleepy town, with one bar, two restaurants, a few cafés, and some shops. It's a fishing village. I frequented the area many times over the six weeks in Morocco, after experiencing the stunning Paradise Valley near Agadir with its amazing mountainous backdrops and fresh water lagoons for swimming. We also spent time in Agadir, Essaouira, Casablanca, and Marrakesh. We found a great town to chill in after experiencing the Medina, which was very interesting to see and experience.

The area we stayed at for a few days in readiness for Jamal's flight home had a great café. It was cheap as chips. Plus, the people were very nice, even though they couldn't speak English. I would sit with them and teach them English and how to pronounce words properly in English. They, in turn, would teach me Arabic. There was a great teahouse across the road. The Wi-Fi would reach to the Beast, so could use it when chilling or in bed.

Because it's inland with no ocean breeze, Marrakesh has crazy humid heat. Fortunately, there was a hamam around the corner.

The time had come for Jamal to fly home. After spending months in each other's company, it felt good to have my own space back again. But I would also miss him travelling with me. The time had come to drive him to the airport and wave him off.

It seemed strange that I was going to lose my travelling companion. But we knew we would always be in touch and plan our next adventure. Seeing him off at the airport with a hug, I wished him a good flight and told him to message me when he was home safely.

I waved as he passed passport control way in the distance. He then turned the corner, and he was gone.

Even though I knew a good friend of mine would be flying into this airport a week later to spend a week's holiday here, it was at that point I felt lost and alone. I left the airport, jumped into the Beast, and decided to go straight to Imsouane to meet up with my good friend Abdou.

On route to Imsouane, I cried. I had just lost my best friend and travelling companion. For the next four hour's drive, I felt sad and alone. I picked up hitchhikers so that I would have company. When I reached Imsouane, it was dusk. The sun looked so beautiful as I reached the crest of the hill, just before the down stretch heading to the town and the beach. It was breathtaking. I stopped the Beast; jumped out; and, just in time, took the picture.

It was a reminder of just how amazing and beautiful this world really was. The picture I took was something you would see in *National Geographic*.

I jumped back in the Beast, flew down the mountain, parked in my usual spot, and went to see my good mate Abdou. He was very pleased to see me back. He was making tagine, a Moroccan delicacy and my favourite. I went up the ladder in the very small but authentic and cosy seaside shack. There was what I called, "The man cave", where we could chill, eat, and relax, with a stunning view of the Atlantic Ocean. This was where I chilled with a Moroccan tea until Abdou showed up with chicken tagine. Abdou is a great cook, and we shared the tagine and chowed down like good Africans do.

After a few hours of chatting and laughing and recalling good old times when Jamal was around, I left him there and went back to the Beast to sleep. It was strange for me just being in the beast by myself. But it was also nice to have my own space again. And knowing Jamal was back in the United Kingdom, safe and on the coach heading back to Wales, I went to sleep happy and full.

The next day, Ayoub, Abdou, and I had arranged a road trip to Casablanca. It was a full day's drive. Plus we had a quick pit stop in Essaouira on route to drop a mobile phone off to a hitchhiker who had left it in the Beast the day before. In addition, I wanted to show the boys the medina and Essaouira, as they had never been there before. So I, the tourist, showed them a city in their own country.

Traditional Moroccan tea pouring

One of the many teahouses

Anyone hungry

Late that night, after a long day of driving but a good day, I dropped Ayoub and Abdou near their homes in casablanca and headed towards the beach for a sleep.

The next day, I decided to head towards Marrakesh slowly, as I would be picking up Helen, my ex, a few days later. She was flying out for a week and I'd said I would show her Morocco. Plus there was something about Casablanca. I just wasn't comfortable there compared to other areas of Morocco.

This is how they roll in Morocco

So heading south inland, I stayed at a few towns, enjoying the local cuisine and culture. A few days later, I was back in Marrakesh with my chums, teaching them English again. It was still stifling hot there. I couldn't wait for Helen to arrive so we could go beachside for the cool breeze.

Helen then arrived late at night from the flight. I picked her up from the airport. It was nice to see her, as we are better friends now than ever before. Plus, the airport here is a really good-looking airport, just like Banjul Airport, The Gambia.

A week flew by whilst I showed her the best places in Morocco and introduced her to all the friends we'd made before she arrived. Helen was blown away, especially with Imsouane, as we all were. I know Helen would live there if not for her work. Plus Paradise Valley really does live up to its name. We also spent time chilling in Agadir, on the beach where Jamal had enjoyed his first camel ride. Plus, using the local supermarkets like Marjane to have a change and buy alcohol, as it's a dry country plus grab European foods.

I must mention that the beach in Essaouira is stunning, especially when the sun his high in the sky and the breeze is blowing. There's a bar there that you can completely relax in and soak up the sun whilst having a little drink.

As I dropped Helen off at the airport, she thanked me for showing her Morocco and said that she had a wonderful time.

I then left, feeling alone again, but manned up and headed south, knowing that I would be heading to The Gambia at some point very soon. Heading inland south of Marrakesh was a first for me, as I'd always taken the coast road. When I got quite far down, the sat nav map seemed to be showing a road heading west right across a mountain. I could have one more night in Imsouane with friends and then say goodbye in the morning for the big drive to The Gambia. But things don't always work out as you plan.

Yes the road was there to drive over the largest mountains of all time. But for the second time, just like in Andorra, the Beast was overheating heading up the mountains. After cooling her down twice, I made the executive decision to get off the mountain, head back to the main road, and just head south to Western Sahara.

Driving through Agadir, the last city before the desert, I stopped at the supermarket to load up on supplies—mainly a lot of water and some snacks.

At this time, even though I'm not a Muslim (but when in Rome), as Ramadan had started, I refrained from eating during the day. But I did drink water as I was driving through the desert, as that is a *must*.

Heading towards Western Sahara, I hit another mountain. Subsequently I stopped before the Beast overheated. Within five minutes a passer-by stopped and said he was a mechanic and his garage was down the road.

I said, "Great. Let's go." I spun the Beast around and rolled down the hill to his garage.

The problem, it turned out, was that the fan wasn't spinning when it needed to be. So the mechanic went to work. An hour later, it was fixed and is still working perfectly seven months later.

In Africa, you will find many toilets that are just holes in the ground with a large white plate surrounding the hole with foot grippers. That way, you can squat over the hole to do your business. It's very primitive, but specialists have proven that this way of excreting faeces is a healthier way.

I had a few Moroccans ask what I thought of their toilets.

My reply would be, after a long silence, "I'm just glad I brought my own."

That reply would always get a giggle, as not many tourists could say the same.

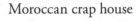

Moroccan crap house

My trip across the desert was something I could never have imagined. I have put myself through a lot, but this was a massive challenge.

Desert road

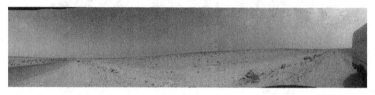

The Beast in the desert

A few empty water bottles from my collection while driving through the Sahara Desert

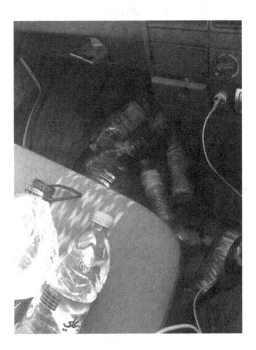

Fortunately, after driving hard every day over sand, sand, and more sand, I would celebrate by buying a nice meal every evening at 8.00 p.m. Luckily, I would find a restaurant or trucker's café around that time, each of which was a Godsend in the middle of nowhere.

One truck stop right in the heart of the desert was a sight for sore eyes. I pulled up, found a good spot to park, and then went in to chow down. After ordering and purchasing, I was seated outside. The wind was blowing hard. The only one sitting out side was me—thanks to the racist server. Much appreciated—not! I was holding on to my food and plates whilst eating so the wind didn't blow it away. The tablecloth, with the help of the wind, was making eating an issue as well. But too hungry to move, I fought the elements and finished my meal. It wasn't the greatest, but food it was. So happy to be full, I went back to the Beast to sleep, as another long drive was on the cards for the next day.

First thing in the morning, I got up, ready to make tracks. I jumped out of the rear of the Beast to get into the driver's seat. I looked around to only see the small café I'd eaten in the night before and nothing else. This was very eerie, as the night before, there must have been fifty or so trucks and the café all lit up like a Christmas tree. In the day, it seemed like an abandoned shack in the middle of nowhere. With that, I set of for the border to Mauritania.

As I arrived at the border, I could see a queue starting to form. Pulling up in the queue, I could see a Mauritanian man getting out of his car in front. He turned around and waved with his arms, signing to me that the border was now closed. At first because this—having a closed border—was all new to me, I hopped out to speak to the gate guards. They repeated what the man had signalled. "The border is closed till 8.00 a.m.!"

I asked, "Can you please open up so I can drive through?"

With no reply and them just muttering between themselves in Arabic, I knew it was a futile question.

I returned to the Beast to lock it. As there was a restaurant and it was nearly time to eat, I walked over. I then could see a sign advertising rooms for rent. I decided to treat myself, hoping the place had air-conditioned rooms with satellite TV. I spoke to one of the guys there who spoke English.

He said, "Follow me."

I followed, and to my surprise, these rooms were not rooms but a big area segregated by curtains, similar to a hospital ward but nowhere near as bright or as clean. Plus the only thing inside these segregated areas were foam mattresses on a concrete floor.

Seeing that, I said, "No, thank you," and walked straight back into the restaurant. All the while, I was thinking, *My motorhome is like a palace compared to what they are offering.*

I ordered the same meal as everyone else, only because that was the only meal that was on offer. Fortunately, it was good and tasty meal. I explained they could bring the food out at the same time as everyone else's, as it wasn't time to eat at the point. I'm very sure the waiter, as there was only one, was impressed that I was partaking in Ramadan; I was the only white man around. After chowing down on a three-course meal, I headed back to the Beast to chill and sleep. I needed to; my belly was over full.

The next morning, with a knocking on the side of the Beast, I was up and ready in no time to get myself ready to cross another border. But this was unlike any border I had crossed previously. With some nervousness, I followed the other vehicles past the large gate into an area where we had to stop again and get out and show documents. The locals pointed out which shacks I had to go into to show my documents. It was a complete shambles way of doing this. We went from one place to another and then back to the same place we'd started. It was ludicrous. Two hours passed with all the queuing, but it seemed like six hours of running around. I had my passport stamped and was allowed to leave Morocco. I hadn't even gotten to Mauritania yet.

That was when the fun started, passing through the Moroccan border and the traffic as we all tried to get through another set of gates, with trucks from the Mauritanian side nudging towards me. This was a complete fiasco. Trucks were barging and pushing. It took an eternity to the pass the gates into what was no man's land for seven kilometres before the Mauritanian border.

No man's land

Note: Mauritania is a no-go country for Brits. The government advises against all travel. But that wasn't going to stop me.

A large amount of people were standing just the other side of the gates in no man's land, asking where I was from and would I want them to show me the way.

I said, "No thanks. I'm man enough to find my own way."

With all that pressure and hustle and bustle, the traffic started moving. I was off, heading towards the Mauritanian border, where all I could see were tyres, broken old television sets, and dumped vehicles everywhere. It was incredible, to say the least.

I followed the truck in front of me, hoping the driver knew his way and just dumfounded that somewhere like this existed. I started to film the surrounding area with my phone to make a video blog. The next thing I noticed was that the driver of a car going in the opposite direction was being very animated towards me and speaking as if I could hear him. The next thing I could see as he drove past was in my mirror; he was turning around.

My first thought was, *What is this crazy guy doing?* Then he sped up to catch me. He actually jumped out of his car and ran over, which was possible as the ground was so bad the top speed I was travelling at was two to three miles per hour. There was no road, just terra firma.

As the guy was running over, he shouted, "Do you have a phone for me?"

I turned around and said, "*No.* I haven't."

He then sulked and walked away.

I was now thinking, *What am I getting myself into?*

After ten minutes or so of crossing no man's land, I saw the Mauritanian border up ahead.

Here was when more corruption was tried, many times. My answer was simple: "I have a visa and was told by your embassy in Rabat, Morocco, that was all I needed to enter, and that if there was any issue, I should call them."

Swiftly the border guards said, "Okay. There you go. Move on."

From that office, I made my way back towards the Beast, where a man was standing with a few pieces of paper in his hand, saying, "There is a border tax."

I laughed and said, "I don't pay tax!" And repeated, "Please speak to your embassy in Rabat over this matter."

After some "er-ing and ar-ing" from him, another guy said, "Come this way."

We headed over to the main office, where they wanted me to scan my thumbprint. I also said no to this. I was then led into the big boss's office, where he was sleeping on his bed. I chuckled to myself. *Wake up, you lazy git,* I thought and slowly sat down onto a chair in his office. I stood straight back up again, fearing it would collapse underneath me; it was seriously rickety.

As we moved back into the hall, many staff members were around, not knowing how to deal with me and conversing in Arabic. I had no idea what they were saying, but the facial expressions gave it all away. Now they had to use force.

So to the Mauritanian sergeant major with the big voice and threatening demeanour came close, I said, "I don't like this man. Can you please step away from me?"

He then replied, "You have gotten away with not paying any taxes. If you don't scan your finger, you won't be allowed to pass into Mauritania."

So I said, "I will do it, but let it be known that I am doing it under distress and harassment."

I then scanned my thumbprint, thanked them, and left.

All I could see were their glares as I smoothly swaggered back to the Beast, happy that I didn't get taken advantage of by the rampant corruption and, hopefully making them think about the error in their ways of treating tourists. It's no wonder that country doesn't have many tourists and is supposedly the biggest slave country in the world. The real largest slave country in the world is the one with the most birth certificates in circulation. Please Google, "Settlement Certificate."

Upon entering Mauritania, still the middle of the desert, I headed towards Nouakchott, the capital city. As it is a huge country and the roads were terrible, it took me two full days of driving to get there. Most of the time, you are off road on the sand, as the roads are blocked. I spent most of the time doing two to three miles per hour on the sand. Any faster in some places and the Beast would have been shaken to bits.

At one point, the road was very good, and I was travelling at my normal speed of fifty-five miles per hour (eighty kilometres per hour). It's a good economical speed. Plus, you get to see what you are passing, which was great in Morocco and in Europe. There is much to see. Here there is only sand, sand, and more sand. At this point, I was staring down a long straight road and a sign in French, when translated, read "Danger 200 metres ahead."

So clearly at this stage, I was scanning the road as well as the horizon, looking for what I thought could be a smashed-up car on the side of the road—something in the road. All sorts of thoughts were going through my mind. But as I was getting closer to this so-called 200 meters where there was meant to be *danger*, I personally couldn't see any danger until—*Noooooooooooooooooooooooooooo*!

I spotted the danger. My ass twitched. My stomach flew into my throat. There it was, a dip in the road. It was too late to brake or even blink. There must have been a drop of two to three feet. That's when everything seemed to slow down for me—apart from my speed—as the beast dropped. I left my seat and flew up into the air. My bum had come so far off the seat that It was touching the roof. I had one hand on the steering wheel, making sure I stayed on the road and in lane, as another vehicle was heading up the other side of the road.

My mind was doing overtime at that stage. I worried that, when I landed again after the first bounce, the Beast would ditch itself sideways in the sand. Or maybe it would land and the Beast would collapse inwards like in cartoons. Then the bounce again came. With both hands now on the steering wheel and trying to settle my bum in the airseat, which was also bouncing up and down, I controlled the Beast and made her stay in a straight line. Then I got my feet back into position so that I would be in total control again after the last bounce. I was hoping everything would be okay. I looked around to what I thought would be a bomb site in the back, only to see that ...everything was perfect.

Only a few kitchen items had dropped onto the floor, including my TV remote control. My asshole stopped twitching as much, and I thought, *What a lucky escape I've had.* I had truly thought I would have to grab my backpack, fill it with essentials, and walk away in the middle of the desert.

Fortunately, it didn't come to that. But I was still concerned about the wheels and suspension. So slowly I stopped. Still bricking it, I jumped out to see if everything was okay underneath.

Thank God it was. By that time in a giggly state, I jumped back into the driver's seat of my trusty faithful and headed south.

Happy to be alive and still have an amazing beast to travel with, I came across a little town. I located a restaurant, parked up outside, and went in for a meal.

I discovered this restaurant had no menus and looked like it would be ready to open to the public in a week or two. The Mauritanian only spoke French and Arabic, so with hand gestures, I asked for, "Food."

With his hand gestures, he said, "Yes, food soon."

With no other choice, I stayed, and we ate together. He brought out fish and rice, of which I'm not a big fan. When the food first came out, I thought it looked like chicken. Unfortunately, it wasn't. But the rice was good, along with a few side snacks. He made a great freshly squeezed orange juice and a milkshake.

Happy with that and with a full belly, I asked in hand gestures for, "The bill."

He then, with hand gestures, replied, "No bill. On the house."

Very delighted with that, I thanked him profusely and left to chill and sleep.

Next morning, I headed for Nouakchott—a very long drive that seemed to have a checkpoint every few miles. At first the military seemed very nice and let me go with no problems. Then the police checkpoints were not so easy.

They would start asking more questions and checking the Beast for infractions, more like corruption officers. Many tried to extort me; All failed. As I was getting asked questions and to show my ID way too many times for my liking, I started to use their politeness to my advantage. When I got stopped, I would say, "I'm in a rush. I have a deadline to get to Nouakchott. Can I pass please?"

Being so polite, they would say, "Yes, of course, sir."

So I would carry on.

By the time I arrived at the last checkpoint just before Nouakchott, it was dark. It was late evening, and I was tired, grouchy, and hungry. Out of the corner of my eye, I saw what looked like a policeman on the other side of the road flashing his torch in my direction. I just kept going, assuming he as flashing me on.

A few minutes later and a mile or so away, I saw this Toyota Hilux pull alongside of me. The man driving was shouting, asking me to, "Pull over," and wearing a very stern look. I then noticed a policeman in the back also flagging me to stop. I was like, Uh-oh. Maybe I should have stopped earlier. Whoops.

I slowed down, pulled over to the side of the road, and waited for the copper to walk over.

As he did, he said, "Did you not see me flashing you to stop?"

In English, I replied, "Sorry, my friend. I thought you were flashing me to pass." Before he had a chance to go nuts, I used my usual blag and said, "I have a deadline and need to be in Nouakchott. I'm very low on fuel. Can I go please?"

The next words he said were priceless, and he would possibly be the only policeman in the world to say them after he had chased me down the road for a few miles: "Of course, sir. Carry on!"

Flabbergasted, I drove on. I filled up the Beast, as was well needed by then; located a great restaurant; and chilled with a well-deserved spaghetti bolognaise.

I must first mention how Nouakchott looked upon entering. It was very eerie, as everyone in the city was wearing the same clothes and they were all so polite—oddly polite (something I'd never thought I would say, but it was true). Not only was everyone wearing the same Mauritanian outfit, but the clothing was also the same colour of blue. It was very bizarre and very odd to see.

After I had eaten, it was time to sleep. So I located where the ocean was by asking many people and headed in that direction. The way people drove there was also crazy. They would drive anywhere the ground was flat, regardless of which way they work going. Plus, to make things worse, they would block the perfectly good roads so you had no choice but to use any piece of drivable terra firma you could—which was pretty much everywhere, including right up close to the buildings.

Feeling like I had just stepped into the twilight zone, I found a long deserted road so decided to turn around and park for the night.

This was definitely the worst night of my life. Mosquitoes harassed me with their buzzing and biting. The humidity was so high it was stifling. On top of all that, I was confronted by what I could only imagine was a car with a very loud sound system. I could hear it well before I could see the car. Slowly, it came closer and closer. I watched from the sunroof above my bed thinking, *Please do not stop. I don't like this twilight zone country!"*

The car then went even slower as it approached. I was very much on edge by this time, my nerves completely shattered. With its eerie passing speed, the loud car went past. It didn't have any taillights either, making me even more wary of this country and its driving habits. Eventually, after what seemed like an hour, the music volume from this car became so low I couldn't hear it anymore. Thank God, the car had gone.

I lay down to try and sleep utterly tired, scared, and agitated. It's very rare I get scared, but here was another matter. I really needed to sleep and leave this country ASAP, as I was not feeling comfortable in anyway.

After trying to kill the many, many mosquitoes, I started to drift off, only for my fears to come flooding back with the loud sound system of that car heading back towards me. It was around 1.00 a.m. and pitch-black. The car was now heading towards me. My fear was even more heightened when I looked out to see that the car was heading towards me with no front lights on either; I only knew that it was getting closer at an eerily slow speed again and music I had never heard before was getting louder and louder.

I then prayed, "Please don't stop."

As the car came closer, I was getting really worried. The car then slowly, slowly, still in complete darkness with no lights on at all, drove past and away.

After that, it was so hard for me to sleep. And with every mosquito I killed, I hoped it would be the last. I would lie down and try to sleep, only to be awoken again with another couple of mosquitoes buzzing around my ears. This went on until dawn. That was when I'd had enough and decided to get my Senegalese visa and move on.

Dog-tired, I drove to find the Senegalese embassy. Locating with very little fuss, I went in to find out the protocol for acquiring a visa. It was now done online. So off I went to an Internet café to fill in the online form, pay the fifty euros from my visa card, print off the completed form, and take it back—very simple and easy.

After waiting I had my picture taken. One of the embassy staff said, "Come back in a few hours to pick up your passport with the visa attached."

So I left, had lunch, and returned to pick up my passport with my new Senegalese visa attached. Boom. Happy times. I could now leave this country—but not before a Senegalese man who had given me a helping hand to get my visa in a timely manner asked me in a desperate way, "Can you please take me to Senegal?"

My answer was, "Sorry, no. My policy is not to take passengers."

With that, I left very quickly, jumped in the Beast, and headed for the border.

As Mauritania is such a large country, I thought there would be more cities and towns. But no; the country was very sparse and very eerie, with only checkpoints and one or two villages on the long drive south. I spotted a few families living in marquees oceanside. But the cliffs to the ocean were so high the only way they could eat here was to fish with rods that seemed to have the largest reels in the world—crazy long.

The last checkpoint before the Senegalese border wasn't as easy as all the others I had come across in Mauritania. These guys were adamant they wanted details. As none of them could speak English, they asked a passer-by (a local English teacher) to interpret and translate for them. At first they were very polite and would put up with me asking as many questions as they were asking. Twenty minutes went by with them not getting anything from me except questions. One policemen was ready to give me his details in exchange for mine, which I thought was very fair. But another policeman out of uniform snatched the piece of paper he was writing on out of his hands, spitting venom towards him. This guy was getting very menacing and loud.

As he was shouting, I said to the interpreter, who was a nice guy, "I don't like that man. He is rude and menacing, not peaceful at all."

He then explained to the others. They tried to control the one getting angry, but he was still going on one. I leaned back in my seat, switching my engine off. I knew I was going to be there for some time and wanted to save my fuel. I remained where I was, blocking the road. I hadn't pulled to the side as they had wanted. I was not going to give them jurisdiction over me.

The banter kept going. After a short while, I knew I had to give them something in order for them to release me from my detainment. I had asked them many times, "Am I still being detained?" Every answer was, "Yes."

Then the request was for me to open the back doors so they could see inside. I thought about it for a minute and then said to the interpreter, who was a nice guy and a very patient man, "I will open the back as long as I can leave after I do so."

He relayed the message, and the reply was, "Sure."

I replied, "I'll give them a metre. They will take a mile. I'll bet you!"

The expression on his face said, *This guy is either crazy, or he is genius—or maybe both.*

With that, I leapt out of the Beast and onto the road, pointing out that I was only doing this under duress. I walked to the rear and opened up the door, showing the two coppers that it was only a motorhome. I repeated, "I'm on my way to The Gambia as a tourist."

I locked the boot and then proceeded back to the driver's seat. After jumping back in, I received the same question they had been asking earlier. "Papers please?" It was like some sort of dated German war movie.

I acknowledged to my interpreter that this was the mile they were after. Then I repeated myself; they are wasting my time. "What law says I have to provide you with any papers?"

Dumbfounded, they knew they weren't getting anywhere. They all had a discussion and decided to take all the details they could—from make of vehicle to the number plate, the description, and colour. After they did that they said, "You may now go."

The interpreter asked me very seriously (after giving me a look like that said, *This guy knows his shit*), "Why were you being like that?"

My reply was, "It's my right to ask questions."

With that, he looked at me with an enigmatic face. I then thanked him for his time and patience and wished him a good day.

He replied, "It was nice meeting you. Have a safe journey."

I started the Beast, waved to the police officers, and told them to take care and be nice. With a big smile, I pushed down on the clutch, moved the gear stick into first gear, and pulled away and waved goodbye. The looks on their faces asked, *What the heck just happened?* I headed towards the Senegalese border.

I arrived very late and parked right in front of the gates at the end of what seemed like an estate—houses and shops, mostly quiet and closed. The only people around were the military and a few locals. I got chatting with the locals and mentioned I had a massive mosquito problem. Anyone from Africa would understand that those pesky tiny insects are not just annoying in every single way, they are also killers killing one person every thirty seconds. Mosquitoes are a massive killer in many countries around the world.

Fortunately, one of the guys I was speaking to mentioned a spray I could buy that would kill them. Needing a good night sleep, I would try anything. I went to the shop and bought a spray can labelled "BOP". This was the first time I had seen this spray. I was told to close all the windows and doors, spray the can's contents liberally all around, and then leave for ten minutes or so. When I re-entered, I was to make sure all doors and windows remained closed. And voila, no mosquitos or any flying or crawling insects, alive anyway. I followed the instructions and left it fifteen minutes whilst we conversed across the road sitting on rocks.

After chatting, I decided it was time for me to sleep, as I was going to cross another border the next morning. I jumped into the Beast and immediately gagged for air. That spray was incredibly potent. It was getting into my lungs. Accchhhhhh. Ahhhhh. Haaaaaaa. It was horrible.

After a while, though, it wasn't so bad, and I got my head down with no mosquitos. Thank God.

In the early hours of the morning, after having had only a few hours sleep, a knock came on the Beast. I knew soon they would open the gates but had no clue to what was going to happen that day.

I got up, washed, and changed and jumped into the driver's seat. I was the first to pass through the gates. After passing through, I could see there was a ferry to Senegal.

After running around for an hour and paying taxes (more like getting legally robbed) and being required to get insurance for fifteen days, I was waved onto the ferry. I made it onto the very rickety ferry with a splash through the water. The ferry could only hold around five cars, including mine, and around 200 foot passengers.

We were away for a very short crossing. After only ten minutes, we were over. I was then shown where to park. I had two corruption artists with me. As I tried to communicate my way through the border. it was sweltering hot and humid. I was extremely dehydrated at this point and was finding this border, the people, and the situation very difficult. I felt like I just wanted to get away from there very quickly. It looked like and was just a very poor port, with a few raggedy buildings and offices enclosed by the river and high walls with barbed wire tops.

Sweaty and dehydrated at the border

The Mauritania to Senegal ferry

I was being harassed, because my vehicle was older than eight years old, I could not take it into Senegal. But knowing my capabilities, even dehydrated and a little disorientated, I was going through Senegal with my Beast. That was my plan regardless of what anyone was telling me. I was not going back through Mauritania at all.

I was given the option to drive through Senegal with a man sitting in with me, as well as an escort to follow me through Senegal—straight through. There was to be no stopping. I was to head straight to the Gambian border. In addition I was to pay a 300-euro bribe. I knew that was ridiculous, and I wasn't going for that at all. My proposition to the port chief face-to-face when I finally got to see him was, "I have a three-day pass, so I can at least see some of Senegal on route, with no escort in anyway."

He said, "No chance."

I then mentioned 300 euros, and he confirmed on paper that I had my pass. He then made me sweat waiting for his answer.

Five minutes later, I got the okay and a confirmation letter stating I could pass freely for three days. We completed the transaction, and I was away. disappointed I had been swindled by corruption. But I was happy that I was through and the Beast was with me. Before I'd left, I had been shown other vehicles that were still at the port. They were older than eight years old, and the owners couldn't afford to pay the corruption fee. The cars had been left, and the amount of ingrained sand proved they had been there for months. There were some very good cars too. Surprisingly, even though the eight-year rule was enforced, the actual cars driving around in Senegal were falling apart. Mine seemed like a brand-new vehicle compared to these scrapyard cars that were, amazingly, still going. It was very bizarre. As was the Senegalese way of driving, which was also scary.

After leaving, I was very happy to be on my way again—until the first checkpoint. I was like, *Not again!*

The checkpoint was 200 yards from the port. I pulled to the side and ran over with my confirmation form the chief, expecting to be on my way again very soon.

No such luck. This was Africa. I showed the form and my passport to the police officers, who could not speak English, only French. With us both acknowledging quickly that we could not communicate, it was down to hand gestures. They flagged for me to sit down. I stayed standing as they pointed to the floor outside their derelict shack containing a locally made wooden table to hold paperwork and mobile phones. Also there were two locally made, shoddy wooden stools and a foam mattress for them to sleep on.

After ten minutes had past whilst they shouted on the phone and to other local travellers passing the checkpoint, they mentioned with hand signals and by pointing at the confirmation letter that it wasn't stamped by the port authority. So returning and feeling unimpressed, I headed straight to the chief's office and insisted he stamp it quickly. That way, I could be away and not to return, ever. That's how annoyed I was with his incompetence.

I then drove quickly back to the police checkpoint. Thankfully it was a yep from the police officers. They gave me a hand gesture and told me to go on through, and I was away—onward and upward.

Dakar here I come. Boom—twenty-second country.

All I could think about on route through Senegal was, *I will treat myself to a hotel, air conditioning, satellite TV, and a scrumptious meal.* This was as far as I was going to get, as it was getting dark. And from what I had seen and bought, currency here was CFA franc, and everything was very expensive.

I sought the help of a local on a motorcycle, who had just finished filling up with petrol. I asked, "I'm looking for a hotel?"

He said, "Follow me."

Awesome, I thought, so followed him for five minutes through the dark town with only street lights lighting the area.

He pulled into the hotel car park, hopped off his bike, took his helmet off, and waved for me to follow him in. I then parked next to him, shut the Beast off, grabbed some cash, jumped out, and followed him into reception.

There, he spoke to the hotel manager in French about me and then said, "Goodbye."

I thanked him, and he was gone.

The place seemed like a clean and quality hotel.

"Yes, sir." The hotel manager greeted me. "How can I help you?"

I asked, "A room please for one night?"

"Yes, sir," he said.

We went through the formalities, with pleasant greetings, and then I was given a key and was shown to my room—a pleasant-looking room, clean and tidy.

My hotel room ritual came next:

> Television on – check
> Music station on – check
> Undress and walk around naked swinging my bits – check
> Turn shower on – check
> Grab iPhone and connect to the Wi-Fi – check
> Sit on the toilet whilst checking my emails, messages, and notifications – check
> Jerk myself off to Pornhub – check
> Shower – check
> Scan through the channels on the TV wearing the hotel's towel wrapped around me and lying on the freshly made bed – check
> Contemplate heading to the restaurant for an awesome and well-needed meal – check
> Pick up my iPhone again, checking and replying to messages and notifications – check
> Get dressed to go to the restaurant –check
> Leave air con, TV, and lights on whilst I go for dinner – check
> Tap pockets to make sure I have my iPhone, wallet, and keys before leaving the room – check
> Leave the room and lock the door – check

After all those checks, I headed to the restaurant. I sat down and asked for the menu three times and a glass of water twice. Looking around, I saw the place was clean and tidy. The carpet was red, the oak tables were well made, the tablecloths were also red, there were long heavyset red curtains to match the carpet also. *Very nice*, I thought, considering we were in Africa.

Eventually, I had my water and the menu. I perused the menu for a short time and decided it was going to be a steak night, so I promptly ordered.

Soon I was sitting back, relaxing, and communicating online, with, what started to be only a few other diners. That moment changed when, what seemed to be like, a young female hockey team arrived. *Noooooooooo*, I thought. *Here comes the noise.*

I enjoyed my food but not the *loud* ruckus that was coming from the table of new arrivals—forty strong women, along with coaches and team managers.

I thoroughly enjoyed my steak, made perfectly by a very competent chef, whilst swigging down two local very nice lagers. Then I paid and left, escaping the screeching of young American girls around fifteen or sixteen years old.

I swiftly left the hotel, just to pick up clothes and essentials from the beast to use until the morning. Then I locked the beast and heard, "Hello. Where are you from?"

I quickly turned around to see where this softly spoken but forthright male voice was coming from. I turned to see a sandal seller right in front of the beast. He seemed to be in his fifties but had the aura of being around eighty, though healthy and active. I replied, "Hi. I'm not in any need of sandals. Thank you."

On closer inspection, I could see these sandals were crafted by an artisan. His make shift shop was outside the hotel on the pavement, with a locally made table filled with more sandals than I could see.

I walked towards the shop so I could look closer at the very well made handcrafted sandals, he repeated, very softly, "Where are you from?"

I replied, "I am from Wales. How are you?"

He said, "I am fine. You have travelled a long way!"

The small talk went on for a few minutes, with him trying to persuade me to buy sandals.

I told him he had some very nice sandals, but they weren't for me. "Thank you anyway!"

I knew I had seen a pair I liked, but I wasn't going to buy until the morning. So I said, "Goodnight," and left to return to my room.

I slept very well, knowing I needed to wash and clean my motorhome very soon to make it again comfortable to sleep and live in—given the sweat, sand, and bugs, especially the mosquitoes.

The next morning, feeling fresh and revitalised, I paid for the hotel, which was a European price—very high compared to prices in other countries in Africa. But I paid, knowing it was worth every penny.

The next morning I left the hotel, and to my amazement, the same guy was still working at the sandal shop. He must work twenty-four hours a day or somewhere close to that. We communicated in a fun and a carefree way whilst I purchased a lovely looking and comfortable pair of sandals. Still to date, the sandals look and feel as good as they did the day I purchased them, even after having worn them for many miles — walking and driving here in the Gambia and in Senegal. I bartered with him down to an agreeable price, shook hands — paid, and left for Dakar.

Dakar had its own surprises—fun ones as well as disappointments.

The road to Dakar wasn't the best, so I travelled at slow speeds again. The roads were rough, and closed roads meant driving to the side on yet again undrivable terra firma. As I drove, I grew increasingly hungry, hot, and uncomfortable due to the heat and humidity. I headed to the Big Smoke.

On arrival, Sunday afternoon, I searched for a money exchange. Fortunately one was open right next to the large commerce building right in the heart of Dakar. At first, I offered to exchange Moroccan dirhams, but the exchange wouldn't accept them for some strange reason. I then exchanged euros to CFA franc, as I had used much CFA already.

On leaving, I decided to find a bar for a few drinks and to work up an appetite for food, which wasn't really a problem, as I was still fasting until 8.00 p.m. every evening. That's when I would treat myself to a special dinner of my choice—something to look forward too.

I left there hunting for a European bar, only to drive three streets away to ask a mechanic in a petrol station for directions. He asked a colleague and then jumped into the passenger seat and points forwarded.

Okay, I thought. *That's how they give directions here. Nice one.* I was thinking maybe we were doing each other a favour. Maybe he was finished for the day and I was taking him halfway home or so whilst he gave me directions.

Nevertheless, on we went. Keep in mind, Senegal is a dry country just like Morocco, but they do have watering holes for travellers or holidaymakers. I can't think why there would be many holidaymakers here. Just like in Mauritania (and opposite to both Morocco and the Gambia), the Senegalese didn't make it easy for anyone to visit their country. So after we had gone down one street, my passenger knew he had gone the wrong way. So we spun around and headed back. Then he leaned out the window at the junction we had just come through to speak to the guy driving the car going past us and get what I hoped was the directions to the bar.

He then indicated that we should go to the right. We headed down around the one-way system to where I had previously changed money and then pulled up a stone's throw from where I had parked. I reversed into the spot close to where he was pointing to. I parked, turned the engine off, and exited the vehicle. Making sure all was locked up and surveying the area, I followed him into the bar, with him still muttering to me about getting me a girl.

"No thanks," I kept telling him. "I'm just looking for a beer and a place to relax with air conditioning."

We entered the bar. I was well happy, as the place looked just like a European bar, with beer and lager pumps and an array of spirits shelved behind both bars, nice new lighting, and a good quality ash bar and tables. Everything looked very clean and brand new. At first, I notice the outer bar had ashtrays and the inner bar behind French doors had none. So I breezed through the doors to the nonsmoking bar. Happy times. I was feeling cool and relaxed. I sat at the bar, ordered a pint, and checked out what was happening on the big screen.

Keen to take the first swig, I savoured the taste by swilling the heavenly drink around my mouth before letting the nectar of the Gods swill down my throat. Ahhhhhhhhhhh, perfect.

With my direction giver sitting two stools away at the bar, I offered him a drink. He politely refused and mumbled, "Do you want a girl?"

I replied, "No thanks. If I need one, I shall pull my own."

With that, he communicated with the waitress in what seemed a friendly way, as if they knew each other.

I savoured the taste of the Gods once again. *Ahhhhhhhhhhh, heaven*, I thought.

Watching sport on the TV and with the air con now on me, I felt very relaxed and comfortable.

I offered my chum again, "Would you like a drink?" After all, he had shown me the way.

His reply, "No thank you. But I will need taxi fair."

"No worries," I said, and passed him enough in CFA for a taxi.

He was happy with the amount, which wasn't a lot, and off he went, leaving me to relax and sink a few cold ones. Happy times.

A few bevies later, and I was communicating with a couple on the table next to me—an old man and a young woman (African love comes to mind) After bantering for a short time, I realised they weren't together. He was the owner, and he left, leaving the pretty young girl behind. She kept talking with me and got me engrossed in a conversation with her, which was very difficult—not.

Time was ticking, and I was getting hungry. Then she mentioned that she knew a great restaurant and she would show me where it was. I knew it would cost me a meal, but I didn't mind so much, as she was good company and attractive. So I paid the bar bill, and we left.

On route to the restaurant, she said her sister was in the bar next to where we parked, and she wanted to see her quickly.

I said, "That's fine."

We both entered the bar after I'd locked the Beast and made sure everything was secure. She seemed a very nice girl. It was a very busy bar. It looked like a typical Welsh bar with a multicultural clientele. I sat at the bar and ordered drinks while she was speaking with and introducing me to all her friends. Time flew by, filled with chatting and laughing with many of the patrons, including her sister and friends.

Just before 12.00 p.m., I decided to go find a restaurant where I could eat. I was very hungry and getting very tired.

The girl said, "I'll show you."

"Come on then," I said.

We then said our goodbyes and left the bar.

She wanted to take a taxi to a restaurant. I didn't. So I went into the restaurant across the road. At least I would be near my Beast and would avoid going somewhere I didn't know.

I entered the restaurant and sat down to what was a huge display projected on the wall. I'm not a huge fan of football, but it was entertaining enough. It was a very expensive restaurant, which was clear from its look. At that time, the girl and her sister entered. *Damn*, I thought, I was hoping to have lost them, knowing it would cost me.

Concerned that they probably hadn't had a meal that day, I let them sit and eat with me.

After eating another fantastic meal and watching the match, I decided to hit the hay.

She asked if she could join me in the Beast. Having a heart, it was hard for me to say no. So she subsequently joined me to sleep in the Beast.

She had seriously gotten herself attached to me overnight as she wanted to come with me to The Gambia. What kind of crazy Senegalese logic was that?

I told her many times, "No. That's not possible."

She kept on and on in the basic English she spoke.

I tried dropping her off at her home, which she didn't give me directions to. So now I'm wondering if she will ever get out. This was taking a toll on me already, and it was first thing in the morning. So I threatened her with just leaving and heading to The Gambia. She would have to make her own way back.

She was unfazed by this.

After twenty minutes of trying to persuade her to get out I said, "Fuck it. Let's go!"

As I was now wound up and stressed, I tried to find the highway out of there but ended up driving around in circles for a while. I located the highway just as I picked up speed I then had to slow down and stop at the tollbooth, still giving her every possibility to leave. She didn't even move a muscle. If there was a bomb underneath her seat I still believe she wouldn't move, she would still have sat there. I gave her plenty of opportunities.

I then paid the toll and drove through, I drove about a mile and then pulled over again, really pleading with her to get out. It wasn't that I wanted her to get out on the highway, but I didn't want to take her so far away from her home town she couldn't get back either. Fortunately there was an embankment to a local road where she could make her way home,

Stuck between a rock and a hard place, I tried to get her out again for another ten minutes. She still sat, not budging. So I give her an ultimatum: "Get out or make your own way back from The Gambia, which is a two-day drive away."

No reply. As tacit is agreement in law, I drove on.

Leaving the highway two tolls down, we were back onto the worst roads of all time. That meant our speed slowed to a crawl, it was a long drive to get to Kaolack. On arriving — evening time, tired, hungry, sweaty, and stressed, I tried to locate a hotel that would except my visa card, as I needed to relax in a fresh room, with air con and a hot cooked meal.

The complications of finding a hotel that took visa was a nightmare. as it was Sunday, it was also difficult to locate a Western Union for a currency exchange.

Fortunately, at my wits' end, I located a hotel right down at the bottom of one of the side streets. The concierge knew of a guy who could exchange cash. He called to confirm, whilst we waited in reception.

A few minutes later, the concierge came over and asked how much I would like to exchange. I said, "one hundred pounds please."

He said, "That's fine. He will be here shortly. Would you like something to drink?"

With a sigh of relief I said, "Yes please," and ordered drinks for us. I asked for the menu also.

The exchange was sorted very quickly. I paid for a room for the night and ordered from the menu for us, I couldn't let her go hungry.

That evening I left the concierge enough money so that the girl I was with could take the bus home the next morning also enough money for her lunch. I planned to be gone early in the morning and could not leave her stranded or hungry.

So that night we ate like royalty and chilled, watching satellite TV in the room.

The next morning I was up and out early, confirming with the concierge that he would make sure she got to the bus, with money and food for the journey. He swore he would do it.

Happy with that, I left for The Gambia.

The road past Kaolack was fine for a few miles, and then it went back to dirt roads. All of a sudden, the tarmac would just end and, you'd back to roads that really needed a four-by-four. But fair play to the Beast, she was awesome. I have never owned a vehicle that had such a strong spirit. She would drive and drive and drive, taking on even the toughest of roads. She could still do the same again immediately with no problems. I, on the other hand, was really not enjoying driving anymore. The roads were that bad. With every metre, every foot, every centimetre of driving that day, I just wanted to stop and not drive, ever again. That was exactly how much I wanted to just, stop.

I pushed on, my blood boiling with every metre I drove. With the sweat and humidity, I was ready to scream.

Sometimes I would come across tarmac, and I would thank God for his mercy. Then just as I would pick up speed and have a cool breeze hit me, which was as refreshing as showering under a waterfall, as quick as it had come, it would disappear. Arrgggggghhhhhhhhhh! Kill me now.

With all that annoyance, I had started to grow a beard, not intentionally. It was itching me like mad. At the next village I passed through, I would stop at a barbershop. *Great*, I thought. Let's stop, have a head and face shave, and hopefully feel better.

I parked the beast opposite the barbers. Straight away on stepping out of the beast, you get some local guy coming up and trying to be your best mate. I spoke with civility to him and headed towards the barber's—a little locally made shack with a mirror, a shelf for blades and trimmers, with two very cheap stools.

At first, it looked busy. But then I noticed there were young girls with very poor communication skills with the barber. I pointed to my head and face, indicating I wanted a shave.

He pointed to his chair and said, "Sit, sit."

I asked, "How much?"

We finally agreed on a price after I bartered with him down to his lowest price, I sat down. He introduced his sisters while he pulled out the cutthroat razor from its sleeve.

The sister immediately says to me, "I love you."

Being that she was no older than fourteen, I chuckled to myself and replied, "I love you too."

She and her friends laughed, and I could feel their eyes burning into my cheek and face while their brother went to work on shaving me. At that point, I came to my senses and realised what a dire straights position I could be in here if he slit my throat. All this was going through my head—a little village in the middle of nowhere in Senegal. My fear was heightened by the remoteness of the area and the fact that no one knew exactly where I was at that point.

We all tried to communicate without much luck, so time was past with laughter, fortunately, at our very bad communication skills. Then the barber finished. I felt my face. It felt smooth. I got up, paid, and left.

I then felt my head, he had missed loads. I turned around, returned to the shop, and pointed out he hadn't done his job properly.

He pointed for me to sit again. So I sat, and he got back to work. Then my fear came back. I prayed he wouldn't slice me up because I had said his work was "very poor".

Luckily, he finished properly this time. I thanked him and left.

Hopping into the Beast feeling a little refreshed and smooth, I head in the direction of The Gambia. Well I was heading south, so I should be heading towards The Gambia.

I was still intent on getting there and staying for a short while. I had made up my mind to sell the Beast, as I had just lost interest in driving on these very poor non-existent roads.

After an hour or so of a hard, demoralising, energy-sapping drive, I came to the Gambian border with relief in my eyes and body. I stopped and jumped out to do yet another border crossing rigmarole—only to be confronted by a whole heap of people insisting I swap currency with them or buy fruit or just trying to bum money from me. I told them all, "*Back up*. Let me deal with passport control, and I'll be back!"

The racism started again, with a few who didn't want to be helpful or just made me wait. The corruption started again, and with my patter, I got it down to a third, just so I could leave the country on good terms. The ranking officer was nice enough to me and peaceful, so he deserved a cold drink out of the money I gave him.

The actual border crossing was composed of a gate that was long width and short hight with many jack built outhouses. After dealing with the Senegalese side of the border crossing, I had the unfortunate task of dealing with the pressure of currency sellers, fruit vendors, and beggars. I firstly gave the beggars some money and then went and bought some apples and bananas. Then I went in for the big transaction—currency exchange. A man and woman fought over who was going to do business with me.

I said, "Pipe down. Who has the best deal?"

Apparently the woman did, so I dealt with her—even though they were all together with the blag of being separate. I told them how much CFA I had to swap for dalasis. I kept a hold of my money until I had agreed the exchange was fair. They then gave me the dalasis to count and see if it was correct. To start with, it was wrong. So I passed the money back, knowing these were con artists. I could see the one count in front of me, and then blatantly, whilst saying, "It's correct," he placed a good few notes into his back pocket. Fuming over this attempted fraud, I ordered them to step back away from the vehicle. They then were arguing amongst themselves, as they had been caught out. I raised my voice to ask them again to step back. They moved away very slowly. I closed the door, infuriated at the cheek of these scammers.

I drove to the gate, which was raised for me to enter The Gambia.

Boom. Twenty-third country. I was very happy to be here but had no time to celebrate just yet. That would come a few days later, when I would reach Senegambia—just like, my soon to be good friend Simon Fenton calls senegambia —"vegas," (more on vegas later.)

I then had a not so fun time at the Gambian border. I showed passport control everything they needed to see—passport and logbook (vehicle details). Then they had one of the drug enforcement officers search the Beast. He looked around inside for a minute and said, "That's fine."

I locked the Beast up, and went back inside with him, for the police to try and swindle me for a hundred dalasis, which was worth around £1.30. "Not a lot," I hear you say. But with me, it's the principle. How dare these guys ask me for money when they get a wage and their job is to enforce common law, not to harass tourists or members of the public?

Peacefully I asked, "What law says I need to pay this fee?"

Then some real BS came out of this policy enforcer's mouth—BS that, from his micro-expressions, it was clear he didn't believe either. I started to laugh at the extreme audacity of this guy. He looked at me is if I knew exactly that he was full of BS and then decided to speak in his mother tongue to his colleagues. They all started to butt in. This banter would go on for another ten minutes, with them not knowing how to deal with me. Then they sent what was perceived to be their sergeant major, who tried to shout me down with intimidation and bullying tactics. I stood my ground. He then asked for my passport again, and he started to threaten that he would take my Beast around the back and strip it for drugs. I mentioned that his colleague had already checked for drugs. He went on and on as he walked out towards my Beast with these threats.

"Are you going to pay or are we going to strip your vehicle?" he shouted, still trying to intimidate me.

I replied, "Your colleague has already searched the Beast. What is your problem?"

He then turned and stormed off towards their makeshift police station, where they did have cells and people locked inside.

At this point, I was getting extremely annoyed with how I was being treated. A moment later, another policemen came from their hut and said, "If you would like your passport back, it's going to cost 400 dalasis."

Still fuming, I said, "If you bring my passport to me, I will give you 200 dalasis, and that's it. Final offer." Being completely pissed off with these corruption artists, I would be happy just to get my passport back and leave.

Shortly, the same man arrived with my passport. I gave him the dalasis with a disgruntled look on my face. He then gave me my passport and asked me nicely, "Please don't mention this to anyone."

I laughed, got back into the Beast, and drove away. The cheek of it. They knew they were doing wrong, but they still did it. Materialism is rife, even in a country renowned for its religion—the irony of it.

Leaving there, I pushed on towards Barra to catch the ferry to Banjul. On approaching the ferry terminal, I could see there was a queue. So I pulled up behind the queue and jumped out to enquire where to purchase the tickets to cross.

Fortunately I bumped into someone, a friendly guy who said he would help me get across. There would be no charge for his services. He worked for the ferry company." *Happy times*, I thought and said, "In that case, lead the way."

I followed him to where I paid through a window at a building with no queue. Things were looking up. I was able to pay in CFA and not dalasis because I was taking my Beast over. Odd reason, but hey.

Then my now good friend asked me to bring the Beast closer, as now I would be the first one on. *Boom*. I shot off to bring the Beast closer. When I returned, I parked at the gate in first position near the military guarded gate. Very shortly, the military let me through to the long and narrow queuing area for the ferry.

I was then told, "Park at the front nice and tight to the wall, so the departing vehicles can pass in the morning."

I was a little disappointed with that news. I had been hoping to get the ferry over that evening. But it was getting late, and I was feeling hungry. So I parked the Beast and was happy that it was safe and secure and ready for the ferry first thing.

I then asked my good helper, who was on the ball, "Where can I buy some food?"

He said, "Follow me. There is a great restaurant that's still open just above where you bought your ticket."

A casual walk back up past the military guarded gate and back out into the town. It was thriving. Loads of people were still working and shopping. There was a large market.

I took a left past the security gate that would be closing as soon as the restaurant closed. We walked around the corner and up the stairs to the restaurant, hoping they were still serving food. Upon walking in, I saw there were no patrons. I then saw some people that looked like staff and quickly asked, "Are you still serving food?"

The reply from what looked like the male chef and female bartender standing behind the counter simultaneously said, "Yes."

With a sigh of relief, I asked for the menu. Seeing that my helper, now friend, had sat down and was playing with his phone, I asked, "Are you hungry?"

His face lit up at this stage, and he said, "Yes, very."

I ordered a chicken and chips for myself. He nodded approval for the same. We both sat down to eat and chatted. he enjoyed my travel stories, and he told me a bit about The Gambia.

After eating, he thanked me for the food, and I said, "Goodnight."

I headed back past the guarded gate and walked down the long narrow area back to the Beast. Along the way, I acknowledged other drivers relaxing with attire (tea) before the ferry crossing the next day.

The Barra to Banjul ferry

The next morning, I awoke to many people talking outside the Beast. Up I got, washed and changed and ready for the crossing.

Many people were trying to sell me things. But the only thing I needed at that time was a local phone number. I was going to sell the Beast, and I wanted anyone who was interested to be able to call me. It wasn't something I really wanted to do. I had become very attached to the Beast. But I had lost the thrill and fun of driving across the unbearable roads. So when, out of the blue, someone came an offered me a phone—a very basic-looking phone at that but nevertheless a phone—I was interested. I made the seller call it so I knew it worked. The earpiece and microphone were fine. So it came down to price.

97

He said, "Okay, 800 dalasis."

I laughed as I always do now. Everyone asks for way more than what he or she is selling (and what he or she will take). I offered 100 dalasis to get a bearing from his facial expressions how low I could go.

We ended up agreeing on 200 dalasis. That was for the phone and SIM card. I had a cable that would charge anyway, so no worries.

After we had waited what seemed like an eternity for the wreck of a ferry to moor and allow the passengers and vehicles to disembark, they, very slowly made their way past and down the long narrow road to Barra and away. Then we were allowed on—foot passengers first with belongings, some balancing precariously on their heads, some with wheelbarrows. Then the vehicles were allowed on slowly. A few cars came barrelling down the road and got on the ferry. So much for me getting on first.

With that, I was ushered to board. I drove forward. The ramps attached to the ferry looked very warn and unsteady. I moved closer. With little worry, I proceeded to board. With the amount of foot passengers adorning the ferry, there wasn't much room for me.

The ferry staff were pushing people back to make room for me to get the whole Beast on board. I eventually got as close as I could to the vehicles in front and turned the engine off—and relaxed.

I looked around at all the people crammed on this ferry, some sitting on benches or the floor, most standing. An older lady asked through my passenger window, "Can I sit in there?"

Pointing to the passenger seat, I said, "Yes of course. Please do."

I helped her with the door, and as she got in, thanking me all the way, I called to the other older lady standing next to her and offered her the other part of the bench passenger seat. She was very grateful also and sat in. Not speaking much English, they communicated to each other the whole time in their local language, which could have been Wolof, Mandinka, or Fula; it wasn't French or English.

After around twenty to thirty minutes, we were nearly ready to disembark. First off were the foot passengers, so the ladies thanked me profusely and stepped out of the vehicle and left. ten minutes later the vehicles started to make there way off the ferry.

Then it was my turn. *Yeeeeeeeee haaaaaaaaaw*, I thought to myself and started the Beast. I was finally on route to Banjul. I past all the craziness of the very busy port and headed into town. About a mile later, I came to a junction. I didn't know which way to go, as I had no real destination in mind. I was just going with the flow, seeing what will happen. I think this is a great approach—who knows where you will end up? Most of the time, you'll find great places and meet great people. This wasn't one of those times, as I shall now explain.

The next thing I heard was someone shouting from the pavement to the right of me for me to pull over. I cautiously looked around, not knowing what to think. And what do I see? A policeman calling me to pull over. I shouted over, "What's up, my brother?" I wore a big smile on my face as I pulled over. *Here we go*, I thought. *More policy enforcers.*

I pulled up and started chatting to the policewoman who was standing on the pavement, and very attractive. "Hey. How are you?" I said.

She turned and, with a cheeky smile on her face, said, "fine fine. How are you?"

Then the policeman, with his copper swagger, strode over and said, "You're not wearing your seat belt. That's against the law. You will have to come with me to the police station and pay a fine.

I laughed and said, "I'm not going anywhere, my friend." I then carried on my conversation with the female copper and told her I was fine, (with a cheeky smile and a wink), "Would you like to have dinner tonight?"

She continued to smile, not knowing what to say. Then the male copper rudely interrupted again and said, "Show me your license, as you will come with me to the station and pay the fine, and I will give you a receipt. Do you understand?"

My reply was, "No, sir, I don't. And I'm not going anywhere with you." I carried on speaking to the lady, who was very keen on me now.

As the male copper left the vicinity, the lady copper said, "How many times have you been to The Gambia?"

I replied, "This is my first time. I arrived in The Gambia yesterday."

Stunned, she said, "No way. You have been here many times before. How do you know our system?"

I said, "I promise you it's my first day here. And your system is no different from many living under common law."

At this point, the male copper, with his bolstered swagger, came back over, asking for my license.

Without hesitation, I pulled it out of my wallet. Here you go, my friend, a piece of plastic with my picture on it.

He was still saying his spiel. "You've broken the law. Do you understand?"

I said, "I comprehend what you're saying, but I don't stand under your authority!" I then went back to further banter with the lady copper, whilst she is subservient to my charms.

Then she said, "You're married and have lived in The Gambia for years."

I began to laugh.

The male copper came back once more, still trying it on. I didn't understand anything he is saying to me, as stated at the start of the book; he had no power over me. He gave me my license back and asked me to drive away.

At that point, I said, "I'm very sorry, but I have business to attend to first." I rolled up my window, casually switched the engine off, hopped out, locked the door, and with a big smile said to the lady copper, "I'll be back shortly. We can then swap numbers."

With that, I crossed the road half dancing with serious swagger as they both watched in amazement. With my fearless peaceful swaggering dance, I made my way across two roads to the phone shop.

I entered the phone shop feeling like the king of the world and proposed a part exchange for the very poor phone I had in my pocket. I made an exchange for a Chinese made, fake Nokia with twin SIM slots and then asked, "Where can I buy credit?"

The clerk pointed across the road.

I left, and with the two coppers still watching in amazement, I put on the same swagger dance, making my way across the road and pointing to where I was going. "I'm getting credit now!" I shouted over.

Still swaggering, I reached the other side and purchased credit.

I then swaggered over the last remaining road of the junction back to the Beast. The lady copper was still in the same place where I had left her. I gave her my phone. She tapped in her number, nothing said, I unlocked the beast, hopped in, cranked the ignition. I opened the window, smiled and waved as I drove off.

I headed down the road to find a newsagent for plain paper and a marker pen to make my sale sign for the Beast. With that swiftly done, I secured the signs in the front and side windows.

Within a few minutes, someone tapped the window and said, "Is this for sale?"

Giving the man a crossed-eyed look, I said, "Yes."

After a while of chatting, I got to know Pako very well. He was my man in The Gambia. He said, "Anything you need, just let me know!"

Pako is a good guy. He did a lot of running around to try and sell the Beast for me. Also, he showed me around the next few days, and I met his mates, also very good guys.

Once I went into town without him, not knowing the local prices and racism that does happen—not all the time, but it happens. The vendors charge you much more than the locals, a lot like in any country really. So you do need your wits about you at all times.

Well this time, I needed an electrical product from a street vendor. I bought one. The price seemed high at the time, but I took it anyway and left. That night, it broke. With that and the mosquitos again buzzing around me making me nuts, I got no sleep again and got bitten to death. I decided at 5.00 a.m. I would book into a hotel that night.

In the day, I met up with Pako and told him this product had broken. He said, "Take me to where you bought it. I'll sort it out for you."

Not needing his help, I took him along anyway. When we got there, all ructions broke loose. The police were called, as the place wasn't going to give my money back. Pako went to war with one guy. As they were speaking Wolof, I had no idea what was being said, but I assumed from Pako's reaction the guy was being racist. Pako went for him, kicking up a right fuss. I told him to calm down. It wasn't helping.

The fact was, whilst all that was going on, I had a replacement item, which I was happy with. "Come on, Pako," I said. "Let's go."

That night, I chilled out in the Atlantic Hotel Banjul, with fresh sheets on the bed and *no* mosquitos, which was incredible. Plus I enjoyed good food in the restaurant, slept very well, and was fresh for the next day.

That morning, I met Pako outside the hotel. He mentioned his friend's girlfriend was interested in the Beast. We headed towards Senegambia (Vegas)—a place I would soon call home.

I then met Mbember and his friend. They both jumped into the Beast, and we drove to see Mbember's girlfriend, Mybrid.

Mybrid was from Denmark and a lovely lady. She was staying at Babula's Apartments in kololi. She and Mbember were toying with the idea of driving back to Denmark when Mbember had his visa.

After chatting for a while, I decided to stay at the apartments myself. This was when I started to fall in love with The Gambia and the way of life here.

Mybrid and Mbember soon became good friends of mine, and I was staying in the apartment next to Mybrid's. We would chat for hours on the balcony between the two apartments.

It was a week before my birthday, and I decided to stay in the apartments until after my birthday, just to chill and relax. The owner, Babula, and his wives were very pleasant and accommodating. I got the room per night for 350d, the equivalent of £3.10 a night. the beer bottles in the bar were 50p each. This was a great place.

Mybrid's father, Karl, only lived around the corner at the time. He is a great guy—crazy, but a great guy. We are still friends to date. We used to have long chats in the bar there—now the chats are everywhere else—about his days as an airline pilot, living in so many countries across the globe.

After chilling in the apartment and bar for a few days, Mybrid mentioned she was going to Senegambia for a few drinks and would I like to join her.

"Sounds good to me," I said.

So the arrangement was made we would leave in a few hours after a shower, shave, and what have you.

We called a taxi and headed for what would become one of my most frequented bar/nightclub (and still is to date, nearly eight months later)—Britannia.

Before I even walked in, an attractive girl caught sight of me. With so much confidence and a little crazy in her eyes, she came straight over to chat with me, asking me a thousand questions in one go.

I said, "Give me a minute. I'll buy a drink, and we can chat soon."

With that, I walked in with Mybrid looking and smiling at me. I was looking back and laughing. We both knew this was going to be one of those nights.

Within a very short time, the crazy attractive girl was back, still asking me a thousand questions in one go. I mentioned that I couldn't hear her because of the music being so loud. She pointed, indicating we should go outside and talk. I thought about it for a second and then nodded in approval, telling Mybrid I would be back soon. She laughed at me as I walked away.

After speaking to Bibi for a short time outside, I determined she seemed like a nice girl but too clingy. So I headed back inside for a few drinks, some laughs, and much dancing. All I remember after waking up in my apartment with Bibi. I was like, OMG! All day I was hungover.

The only way Bibi was going to leave was if I said yes to her picking me up the next day to go to church.

Gambia is full of Muslims, along with a few Christians. It's a very peaceful country.

Plus, they have many bumsters (con men) who will try and blag you to part with your hard-earned money. Blags range from things like, "You live in the apartments across the road from me; everyone says you're a nice guy — can you lend me money until later. blah blah blah. I'm getting married. Can you help towards that? Blah, blah, blah. also, "My wife is in the hospital. We just had our baby, and my wife has breast cancer and can't breastfeed. Can you please help me buy milk? Blah, blah, blah."

After I got suckered in once or twice, I wised up to the blatant blagging. Now, I mostly only help the disabled or old and steer clear of the bumsters. Even after living here for eight months, you still have many guys shout to you from from across the road, "Hey. How's your holiday?"

Then you know the blag will follow after a quick introduction.

Or they'll call, "What is your nice name?"

I say, "What makes you think I have a nice name?"

Kids playing in The Gambia

Gambia has its own charms. It has:
    Superb beaches and weather
Serenity
Peaceful people
Friendliness
A laid-back way of life
Affordability
Food that's not genetically modified
No chemtrails (Geo-engineering)
A clean ocean
Beautiful women

It's bad points include:
        Bumsters (con men)
        Racism (discreet)
        Food (lack of choice)
        Entertainment (too little)
        Thieves (too many)
        Mosquitoes
        And did I mention bumsters?

I spent my birthday at Babula's apartments. I also had my Beast cleaned thoroughly. I moved back into it and moved to the beach, which was great. I felt safe and secure, with security in the restaurant next to me and military stationed at the top of the road.

I got to know the locals and military very well, as I lived there for a few months. I would swim most days, relax, watch movies, eat out, get drunk, and womanise. It was perpetual for a long time. Some girls were good, some thieves, some tinkers. It was there I had my iPhone stolen by a girl leaving first thing in the morning. I lay down to go back to sleep after she left and then two minutes later, after feeling uneasy, I jumped up with a huge hangover, checked for my phones and wallet, and noticed my iPhone was gone. I got dressed in a flash, leaped out of the Beast, and ran as fast as I could towards the military. I asked if they had seen her. They said, "Yes. What's happened?"

I explained briefly when I returned from running to the main road to see if I could catch her before she jumped in a taxi, "Damn, damn, damn!" She had gone with my iPhone, including all my pictures, videos, contacts, and everything else on that phone. Grrrrrrrrr.

That's why I liked Morocco so much. If you get caught stealing, *off with your hand.* Great idea. They should do that everywhere! It might sound harsh, but it works very well as a deterrent.

It's still annoying to date. But you get on with it. And the thieves don't end there. More to come of that later in the book.

There are some very special people from The Gambia and surrounding countries. At one restaurant, which was more like a trucker's café, in Senegambia just off the strip (Vegas strip), I had a great encounter with a waitress. I asked, "May I please have the breakfast with bread?"

Her answer, priceless. "We don't serve bread, only toast."

Gambians—adult bodies, child brains.

Not all, but a lot unfortunately.

One afternoon, I was chilling in the Beast on the beach watching a fantastic TV show called Lie to Me. My good friends Mybrid and Mbember pulled up alongside the beast and stopped. We chatted for a while. It was nice to see them, as I hadn't seen them for nearly two weeks. They had been busy travelling and seeing The Gambia with a car Mbember had borrowed from a friend, which was nice.

"We should catch up very soon," I said.

They were off for food and were going to have an early night, as they were tired from all the travelling they had been doing. So off they went.

First thing the next morning, I had a phone call that woke me up. I looked at the phone and saw it was Mbember. I was very surprised to have a call that early from him, so I answered. "Hello, Mbember. How are you?" He replied, "I'm not good!"

Hearing this and the way he'd said it, my heart dropped. I knew something bad had happened. I then replied, "What's up?"

He paused for a second and then explained. "Mybrid died last night ... She got up during the night with a coughing fit and collapsed. Whilst she was unconscious, I picked her up and took her to the car and rushed her to the hospital."

All this time, I was finding his words hard to comprehend. "Nooooo," I said. "This can't be!"

He carried on explaining. "I took her to the local hospital. and the staff said there were no doctors at that time of night. So I then rushed her to the hospital by the turntable. As soon as I arrived there ...Mybrid was dead!"

I was still coming to terms with what he was saying. I said, "I am so sorry. Mybrid was a lovely lady and a great friend." She was so full of life and looked healthy when I had seen them both the day before. "I'm so very sorry. If there is anything I can do, please let me know."

He said, "Okay. Thanks. Will do. I have a few others to call now."

"Take care, Mbember," I said. "And please stay in touch. Goodbye."

For the next few weeks, I was out drinking and womanising every night—getting so drunk I don't remember getting home. I'd wake up in the bed of some random woman, even though I was technically seeing a Gambian girl, Ndey, who would cook and clean for me. Ndey was and is a very nice woman. We are still great friends to date, even though, once, I woke up in a masseuse's bed. She gave a great massage, so I didn't answer my phone for two days. I just went of the radar whilst she massaged me, we went swimming, eating out, and drinking. We had a great time. Unfortunately, Ndey was frantic. I heard later that she had gone to the tourist police to report me missing. She'd thought I had been kidnapped. I felt very badly that she'd thought that, and it was nice to know some people actually cared for me. I wasn't used to that at all. Ndey and I are still very good friends to date.

One night, the masseuse and I were having dinner in Churchills, a bar on the Palma Rima part of the beach. We finished eating and left to sleep in the Beast in the car park outside. After a short time, we were both lying on the bed touching each other and kissing; one thing led to another, and then we were full-power riding. The Beast was rocking. I was giving it to her like a stallion race horse on cocaine and Viagra. She was sighing with ecstasy. We were really going for it.

Then *bang, bang, bang* on the door. That put a downer on the mood straight away. I shouted, "I'm coming!"

I put on my shorts and opened the door. I saw an adult male shouting at me, saying, "You're going to jail for this!"

"If anyone is going to jail it's you, for harassing me in my private residence!" I told him. I then went on to say, over his voice as he was repeating himself, "If you don't leave, I will call the police because of your harassment at my private residence!"

As he was trying to shine a light inside, I moved his arm away from the door so I could close it and told him, "Go away!"

I then jumped straight back on the bed to carry on where I had left off. Within no time, the race horse was off again.

Then *bang, bang, bang* on the door.

With that, I started to get my hair off with the man I assumed was the security guard from the bar, Churchills. I got up, put my shorts back on, and shouted, "What do you want now?"

I opened the door to two grown adult males, one of them the same man from earlier, still gobbing off. I kept myself cool but forthright and spoke with rhetoric. "What is you problem?" I asked.

The first man kept repeatedly shouting, "You are going to jail for this."

I laughed, knowing this was a complete idiot who had no idea what he was talking about. I asked him, "If you know the law so well, where did you get your law degree from?" I knew full well he didn't have one because he was completely clueless.

At this point, he tried to get into the Beast. Uh-oh. Bad move for him. Out you get. I pushed him out. All the while, he was still ranting about how he was going to phone the police and have me arrested. I laughed and said, "Phone the police. It's you who will get arrested for harassing me in my private domicile. Go away!" I said, Calm and collected, I closed the door.

Half of me hoped the men would phone the police so I could deal with this matter swiftly with no issues for me. Plus it would be nice to see them get a mouthful for being so disruptive and harassing. The other half of me wanted them to leave us alone and mind their own business.

A few minutes later, *bang, bang, bang* again on the door.

I put my shorts on and shouted, "Coming. Keep your hair on!"

I sat on the sofa like I always do to open the door. As I opened it, I saw three to four military men and the same two knob jockeys who had been there earlier.

Before I realised what was happening, one military man jumped in and passed me.

I said, "How dare you step in without my permission or a warrant!"

As I said that, the gobby security guard tried to get into the beast also. He then had me push him straight back out.

I explained to the other military men, "I do not permit this harassing man to enter my domicile and was not impressed by their colleague now harassing my guest!"

I sat and calmly explained to the military men that I was minding my own business in my private residence when these harassing guys started to disrupt my evening. "Can you please call a senior officer here?" I asked.

Whilst the knob jockeys kept raring up, I just stayed cool and calm, not wanting to give the military any problems or a reason for them to detain or arrest me. I am a peaceful man, but I will stand my ground and use my God-given inalienable rights; I knew I hadn't broken any laws or statutes.

The senior officer soon arrived, which was great because he had already asked the question, "Is it a camper van?" That meant he knew it was a private domicile and knew no law had been violated in anyway.

I explained to the very decent officer, "These guys have been harassing us and disturbing our evening. Can you please express my disgust with them over this matter, as we are good customers of this fine establishment?"

He said, "Yes."

Then he went straight into a torrent of what sounded like a good telling off to this knob jockey in Wolof. It left the man seemingly emasculated, which he did deserve. And the officer made him apologise to me for what he had done.

I then replied, "You should be nicer to people, and please don't jump to conclusions again about things you don't have the intelligence to back up!" I left him feeling even more emasculated as he stood there with the expression of a naughty schoolboy.

I thanked the officer for acting professionally. And in accordance with being a gentlemen, I shook his hand and decided to head back to the monkey park side of the beach, as I'd had no problems there at all.

Driving out of the car park, I sarcastically gave the knob jockey a wave and said in a high-pitched sarcastic tone, "Bye, bye now. Stay safe."

The Gambia is a strange old country. It will try and put you down, not just once in some cases but numerous times. Don't let it. And don't trust anyone at all. But sometimes, through all the lies and the scam artists, there is a little light that shines through.

Also, some people still give it that charm —that can only be found in Africa.

TIA (This is Africa).

At present, I'm sitting in my friend's office typing the last paragraph with 8 per cent battery power and no charger lead; at present, I am homeless in West Africa with a grand total off 58 dalasis (around 89 pence). I have one pair of shorts, two T-shirts, two boxer shorts, three pairs of ankle socks, and one pair of trainers in my possession, not forgetting my baseball cap and glasses.

All this is because I sold my motorhome to the buyer in instalments.

I did explain what happened and why it had to go to court also why I was homeless further on in the book but unfortunately I had to redact all for liable reasons. "Sigh"

Ill explain more later on in the book.

A few days, a good friend of mine, Kaddie Jatou Mbah, died in a tragic car accident. Kaddie was only twenty-three, with her whole life ahead of her. She was a really sweet girl, and I had been taking her to a few of the local hospitals to see many doctors, all of which were useless. They could not diagnose why she had been menstruating for four months, and Kaddie was trying to stay strong, even though she had been in a great deal of pain for so long.

I still miss her very much. Kaddie had such a sweet heart.

RIP Kaddie

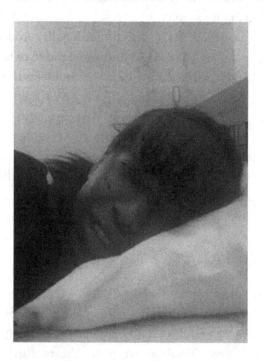

Over the last few months, even though I feel as though I am in limbo, so much has gone on, and it has not been easy at all. The only saving grace is that my good friend Kyle Omailon has been helping me out a great deal and has been closer to me over the last few months than my own family. He has helped me with food, shelter. we drink at Calabash. It's a great place to meet with friends, have cold beers from the ice bucket at only 150d for four beers (the equivalent to £2.13). Plus, the bar is lovely, and the staff are great. We, the league of extraordinary gentleman, meet there every Friday for laughs and games of pool. And sometimes we even put the world to rights.

At first, life got very difficult when I had a blister, from what is called a "blister beetle". I had a blister on my thigh, one on my gonads, and a very small blister on my penis. I was in excruciating pain for about a month. No painkillers were helping, so I suffered sleepless nights and restless days, trying not to scratch (which was very difficult) and in a great deal of pain.

For anyone not in the know about blister beetles, these nightmare beetles, when squashed, splatter their blood, which is like acid to skin. So you can now imagine how painful it can be; it is that painful—*ouch*.

Plus unfortunately, I contracted a rash—an all-over-the-body rash, which didn't help either. It was irritating and itchy. I forgot to mention the blister beetle on my thigh was the same size as a beer mat. I also had small blisters around an inch in diameter across my ball sack and penis; it was extremely excruciating.

That was just the start of my problems over the next few months.
The whole story of the sale of the Beast had been redacted, unfortunately.
Basically, the nuts and bolts of it are...........
The guy I was selling my beast to didn't pay all the payments, in-between the payments I required some where to live so the buyer offered to rent me a room in his compound, bad move on all accounts. as I didn't get all my money for the beast, also I was locked out from my home as we had a big argument as I hadn't been paid the full amount. Thats the reason for me being homeless and penniless.Africa is a very harsh and unforgiving continent especially when you have, nothing.

I have been emailing my estranged father, who lives in, Australia. That is one of my favourite destinations of all time. I have been going there since I was a small boy. My brother and I first went there when I was around thirteen and my brother Arron was fifteen. He was of age to work, and I was of age for school. So for a few months, I enrolled in Richmond High School, which I loved, and made some great friends. I also thoroughly enjoyed taking a tram to school every day and learning with the locals; it was a great experience. Arron worked in the local Ford garage as a technician and took great pleasure in spending his wages—which was understandable, as he was only fifteen years old. Fair play to him, every weekend once, or maybe twice, he would spend his wages on buying us ice cream. That was one of the highlights of my weekend.

My father divorced my mother when I was very young, and we would only see him once a week, if that, for a trip into Cardiff from my home town, Penarth, South Wales, United Kingdom. He would take my brother and I into town, and we would go to the fast food restaurant for a burger and chips. That was about it, and he would then take us home. Only every once in a while, we'd go to the museum or some other attraction.

He very soon after that moved to Israel and once invited Arron and me to visit. I would have been around eight at that time. Israel is a wonderful country, and I had a great time visiting the Wailing Wall, Jerusalem market, Kibbutz, and Haifa.

The first thing that hit me when I disembarked the plane as the steps led straight to terra firma was the smell in the air—completely different from any other smell I had ever smelt. The deserty musky aroma—that is Israel.

Israel is a super interesting country with great history and religion. It's very spiritual. Even as a young boy not into religion, I was taken aback at how religious the Jews were. We weren't in Kansas anymore.

I remember going to watch *Gremlins* in the cinema, which was fun. The Hebrew subtitles were alien to me. I used to enjoy spending time with my father back then and in Australia. But since I grew up he became more estranged, especially when he met his new (and current) wife, Amelia. My brother and I first met her in Israel at the Kibbutz (name redacted). I found the kibbutz great when I was with my dad on the Giraffe (mechanical crane) picking fruit and cycling around the compound with my brother. I used to love playing basketball in the underground court they had—a former bomb shelter I heard.

Once we were asked by my dad, "Where did you get the bicycles from?"

Our answer, "We just pick them up where they lay and use them until we had finished then just leave them."

My dad was furious as we were using bicycles that belonged to other children from the kibbutz.

Whoops.

I'll explain why we thought that would be acceptable. For anyone that doesn't know what a kibbutz is, it's a large compound where people live, off grid. No money changes hands that I know of. Everyone who lives there gets a residence that consists of bedrooms, a living room, and a toilet. There is no need for a kitchen, as there is a large canteen located on the compound, so people pick fruit, grow crops, and generally just enjoy their time in a serene and friendly environment. Everyone has his or her own job—picking, growing, cleaning, or cooking. There are possibly other jobs, but that's research for another day.

Even when we went to Australia to visit my dad, Amelia still didn't want to be civil to us. We met our sister there (name redacted), and soon after, they had another child (name redacted). Our sisters always used to enjoy when we came to visit them in Coburg, a suburb of Melbourne. We did do once or twice as my brother and I got older.

I used to make money in the UK to pay for my ticket and fly to Australia, as I enjoyed the life there. At one point, I was staying with my dad and ran up a huge phone bill, calling mates, including Jon Mcintyre, back in the UK on their mobile phones.

I promised to get a job and pay back the huge phone bill, which I did.

I located a great job, working for a charity. It was cash in hand, and I was collecting money to help disabled people play sports. Fair play to my good mate, Plugga, who was the manager—after I'd been working there for a short time, he arranged for me to keep working without a visa. Thanks, mate.

I paid back every single penny I had spent on the phone bill. I do like to keep to my word.

The main reason I liked working for Sports Federation Foundation was that not only was the staff incredible, but I would also work at my leisure. Being a friendly happy-go-lucky chap, I would get many to donate in sealed tins that I would take to the people, especially busy places, like food malls, the streets, and stadiums at match times.

Once, Plugga and I were collecting at the MCG (Melbourne Cricket Ground). We decided to go in and watch the match between our team, North Melbourne (go the Roo boys), and Essendon, another great Aussie rules side. We took to our seats, nice and high in the stadium next to the rest of the fanatical, flag-waving, pom-pom-shaking Roo boy supporters. It started out to be like any other game. Then a minute in, the first of the goals started to come in thick and fast. It was a frenzied first quarter.

How the games work there is that they only play live on TV when they have a sell-out crowd. This, at first, was far from a sell-out. But after the first quarter, North Melbourne had scored more goals than they normally would in the whole game. Essendon was doing okay with the scores as well, but North Melbourne was way ahead. Word got out of the stadium; in-stadium supporters must have phoned friends and family, as it started to get a lot busier.

Then the second quarter started with a blow of the whistle, and before you could get your breath, North Melbourne scored again. As we were still cheering for that goal, they scored again. They were mostly all unbelievable goals—*Guinness Book of World Records* style kicks, marks, and goals.

You had to be there to believe it. Time flew by, and by the end of the second quarter, the points for Essendon were substantial. But the Roo boys scores were off the charts. More and more people were coming to fill up the stadium. The stadium went from a quarter full at the start to three-quarters full by the third quarter, which was unheard of. The feel of the stadium was electrifying. The crowd was bouncing with excitement; the fans were roaring. You knew you were at the game of the century.

The whistle blew for the third quarter to start. *Boom.* They got straight into it. A throw, a toss, and a kick—*gooooooooaaaaaaaaaaaaaalllllllllllllll* from the Roo boys. They truly were on fire. The points were just building. They were so far ahead, it seemed Essendon would have to score ten games worth of goals to win, which would normally have been impossible. But with this game, anything was possible. Essendon held its own, scoring whenever possible. It seemed at this point there was no stopping either of them, as both teams would score every time they touched the ball.

The end of the third quarter came, and every one could relax and take a well-earned breath. More and more people arrived at this point, and the TV stations started live coverage—setting another precedence—before the final quarter, the stadium was full to the brim. All eyes in and out of the stadium in the whole of Victoria were to watch the final quarter of this spectacular battle between two fantastic sides. We, the North Melbourne fans, were content in the knowing this was our win at that time, as we were miles in the lead. Still, it was such a phenomenally enjoyable game.

The whistle blew for the fourth and final quarter. Essendon went tearing at the Roo boys with everything they had and started scoring some amazing goals. Every few seconds, a kick would be made by an Essendon player, and as if carried by the hand of God, it would fly seamlessly through the air straight between the posts. The crowd *rooooaaaaaarrrrrrreddddddd*.

At this point, it didn't matter what side you were on; just the magnificence of the players and their skills would amaze your senses. Everyone would cheer whichever side scored. It was truly an unbelievable event, especially now Essendon was closing the gap. Every minute that was passing another goal was scored.

It got to the point it could go either way. Tension mixed with enthralled stimulation never felt before or since. It came down to the wire. Who was going to win?

Minutes before the end, Essendon took the lead. It felt like the stadium lifted ten feet. The crowd *rooooaaarrrrreddddd*. It was deafening. Then, with seconds on the clock left, it was an all-out battle for the Roo boys to take back the victory we all believed they had. But as the seconds ticked away to the final whistle, North Melbourne just couldn't cut it.

Still, what a game. Nobody really cared at the end who had won. We had just watched the most impressive Aussie rules football match of all time. The game would be spoken about for months, and years later, it's still discussed and raved about.

That evening in Melbourne, Flinders Street, the Yarra, and Crown Casino had revellers all over celebrating. If your team won or lost, it didn't matter. We all celebrated like it was 1999. Life was good.

Also, I enjoyed working for the charity, as I would get a small percentage of the money I collected. I could survive and keep collecting most days for the charity. Collecting on the trains was great fun. I would walk through the carriages whilst in motion. I wasn't supposed to do so. But I was slightly rebellious, and I was collecting for charity, so no harm no foul. I carried on. I would come through the door to a full but quiet carriage, and with an authoritative, loud, pleasant voice, I would say to the people closest that I was collecting money for charity and I was going to make the passengers at the other end of the carriage smile.

With a big beaming smile, I would shake my tin and let the sound of the jingling coins inside do the work for me. I would keep my eyes peeled for the first person going for change and be on him or her, looking at others to do the same. I didn't expect much from each, but a small gesture was perfect, as it all mounts up.

I would even go travelling with work, as I'd made some great friends. It was like a family I'd never had. We would go all over Victoria and New South Wales to work.

Geelong, Victoria, was a favourite of mine. It was a great surfing village, with beautiful women and one of the best smorgasbords around. For those who have never been to a smorgasbord, it's a real food festival—an all-you-can-eat buffet. Mmmmmmm. My favourite.

I met a beautiful and sweet woman in Geelong one evening. I truly can't remember where we met. Maybe it was in a bar. But I do remember going back to her home. She was around my age but lived with her parents. She invited me to her house. I remember being a little drunk, as was she. We went to hers to have a few drinks from her parents' in-house bar. Bad move. I remember being at the bar having had a drink or two and we heard footsteps upstairs.

She said, "That's my dad, and he doesn't like me drinking from the bar."

Ohhh, great, I thought.

At that point, she grabbed my hand and ran with me in tow across the living room floor. Then I heard footsteps coming down the stairs. *Oh, shit,* I was thinking, as I was dragged running through the side door. We ran all the way to the beach laughing our tits off.

We got to the beach, dropped to the sand, and rolled around laughing. I looked up to the night sky and was amazed at how beautiful it was, with the sound of the crashing waves hitting the beach. With a really beautiful and down-to-earth woman next to me, I was in paradise. We chatted some more and laughed. I was truly in awe of the time I spent with her.

We started kissing and touching each other. We then tore each other's clothes off in an intense but loving way. We made love for what seemed like hours. I felt like a real stallion, as she was coming so hard I became soaking wet. She moaned so loudly I was worried someone would hear. The next thing I felt was the waves crashing against our legs as we climaxed simultaneously. What a feeling; what a rush.

We ran up the beach laughing, pulling our clothes back into some sort of a decent fashion. She grabbed my hand and whispered into my ear, "Let's go back home and finish off my dad's supply of grog."

A bit wary after what had happened at hers earlier and still drunk, I of course thought about my decision for a second. Then I decided. I whispered back into her ear, "Let's do it."

She smiled with wide eyes and a beaming beautiful smile and perfect teeth. She truly took my breath away. Grabbing my hand more tightly, she started to run, again with me in tow.

As we came closer to her house, we slowed down to a walk and quietly made our way up the driveway to the side entrance, listening intently to hear if her father or mother was up or around. The house and the street were silent. the only noise was the crashing of the waves against the beach. As we approached the side door, slowly and silently, we looked straight into each other's eyes. With cheeky grins, we entered her home. I was feeling like a naughty school boy at twenty-five. We very quietly and slowly moved towards the bar. She went straight for a bottle of spirits. I can't quite remember which one, but I was happy with the choice and she poured. Still sporadically laughing about the evening, we clinked glasses and drank away.

That was all I remember of that night. But the next day after I woke up with a killer hangover back at my digs, all I remember was I wanted to go and find her. I forced myself to overcome my hangover, get up, and go and look for her. I explained to the boys where I was going and left. Some of the boys remembered her and said, "How did you pull her?"

I said, "With my sexual magnetism."

We all laughed, and I left.

Fortunately there was no work that day, as it was a Sunday we had off. Unfortunately, I couldn't remember her name or where she lived.

I went searching anyway. As I walked towards where I thought she lived, more of the evening was starting to come back to me.

I walked along the beach and spotted the place where we had made love. I was very happy with that; I knew I was close. I carried on walking, reminiscing the time I had spent with her. I then started to remember things, like her old man shouting at her because we were sniggering and laughing.

I also remembered us starting to get frisky again on her parents' thick plush rug next to the bar. That was the point too much noise was made. A big thud came from upstairs, and a bellowing man's voice shouted, "Who is down there with you?"

She shouted, "No one!" as she shuffled her clothes back on and opened the side door, ushering me through.

I grabbed my clothes at the sound of her father's footsteps coming closer to the top of the stairs and leapt silently towards the side door. In what seemed like slow motion, she kissed me on the cheek and said, "Go. We will meet tomorrow."

The next thing I remembered as I was walking along the beach looking up at the houses where I thought she lived was that I was out of the house like a flash and down the street faster than Speedy Gonzales. In that split second, I had turned quickly to see if I could remember the house, and I was gone.

As I walked up and down the street looking for the house, I realised they all looked similar. In fact, they all looked like the one I had remembered seeing when I was making a hasty getaway. I also put myself off knocking any doors, just in case her father had a shotgun or anything else detrimental to my health.

After an hour or so of looking, I left and went back to where I was staying.

I went to the local bar that night to see if I could see her. But unfortunately, I never saw her again.

Australia has been very good to me. I enjoyed every moment of holidaying and living there. I even outstayed my visa once and had to make the money for my return flight in one week.

My father wasn't going to help me, so I had one week's notice from the Australian immigration department to buy a ticket and leave. Fun times; I can say that now.

At that time, I was squatting in a house in Footscray. It was my mate Plugga's old home. He'd owned it and then sold it to his brother; then he lived in it until his brother sold it. Plugga asked to me one day if I would like to live there; when he moved out, he would leave the keys in the letter box. In Australia, the letter box is outside the house. So he left the keys in the letter box for the estate agent, and I just happened to take them out and use the house. Good on ya, Cobber.

I lived there for a couple of months and even rented a room out to a mate I worked with. We had a great time there. I had local bars and close train stations. I even had a big screen TV, a Nintendo, a nice armchair, and a bed. The electricity and water was on. It was superb. I even had a free train ticket to get back and forth between the city and Coburg. There was a section of track out, so you would have to bus around that track. But I was in Footscray now. Bus link not needed. Plus, my free pass would still work. Happy times.

So my days were spent working, and my nights, either chilling at home or down at the local boozer chatting to friends and playing the local pokies (gambling machines). I'm not a gambler at all back in the United Kingdom, but in Australia, I used to spend so much time in Crown Casino it was unreal. Another reason I moved into the squat was to get away from my stepmother. If she was a nice woman, I would have had no problems with my dad being with her. But she wasn't nice, not to me anyway.

I have so many stories to tell about my time in Aus. But I will move on and get to my point—the reason I started writing about my father—after I finish the story about overstaying my visa.

Immigration went to my workplace, as they had a record of me working for a short time there (before it had been wangled for me to work under another name).

I was left a message that I had one week to vacate the country. Otherwise, there would be serious consequences. Knob-heads.

I then, with no real money to my name, wondered, *What can I do? Should I ask my dad?*

No was my answer to that. Why? Because he wouldn't help me if I was dying.

Even penniless and homeless in Africa my dad only helped me with £200 which was a hardship to even get that amount, which unfortunately didn't help me in anyway.

As my mum had died when I was 17, I had no-one else to ask.

I discussed my situation with the assistant manager of my workplace. I can't remember his name, but he was a great friend of mine—he, his wife, and his kids.

I even stayed at their house for a short time; super nice family. I even went to church with them. That was where I got baptised. I was in my mid twenties.

He said he would take the money from the office safe so I could buy my ticket back to the UK and earn the money within the week to pay it back. I couldn't believe it. He was willing to risk his job and possibly prison so I wouldn't get in to anymore trouble.

At first I said, "That's very nice of you, but I can't put that pressure on you."

He sat me down and explained that was my only option, and he had faith in me to make all the money back in one week. This was a lot of money. I can't remember how many hundreds of Australian dollars it was at the time. But it meant I had to work shitloads and pray it would be enough.

I did get talked into it. That's right. His name was Geoffrey Fielding or Fieldew, something like that. Some people you just want to keep as your friends forever, he and his family were a one of them.

I gave my word that I would do my damnedest to get the money back to him, fast.

I paid for the ticket, which was flying a week Tuesday at 10.00 a.m. from Tullamarine Airport, Melbourne.

Every day, I was at the office when it opened and back just before it closed. I used my knowledge of Melbourne and where I could make the most money in the quickest time. That meant everyone I saw in the street heading towards the city, every food mall in the city. I headed towards Flinders Street train station to ask the passengers on the station platform and then on the trains heading out off the city. I would then come back into the city and hit the pubs and food malls again. Then I'd head to the train station platforms and carriage passengers out of and into the city on many lines, avoiding the guards at all times, jumping trains and passing from carriage to carriage mid journey. Then evening times, I would hit the bars and food malls again until I would go back to the office. I would also be dodging bylaw officers day and night, as I had not only no permit to work those areas but no work visa. Whoops. Ha ha. Shit happens.

Knowing what I know now, that wouldn't bother me in anyway. I must have had the common sense to realise that years ago. I wasn't breaking common law at all, just government (Mafia) rules and regulations. Fuck 'em. No one got hurt.

So that was my day every day until Thursday morning. As I was watching TV before I left for work, my flatmate came in from the kitchen, saying, "There was someone here to see you."

Very bewildered at his statement, I was taken aback. Anyone who came to see me would phone first. A second later, he said the same thing.

I got up and walked towards the back door, as that was the only door we used. That's when I saw a suited man come through from the kitchen towards the living room. I asked, "Who are you and what do you want?" Please remember, I had been squatting there for a couple of months and had no strange visitors.

He said, "You are not supposed to be here, and you should leave." He showed me his business card from the estate agency where he worked.

"I cannot leave today," I told him. "I have looked after the place for months. No walls have been put through. There is no damage, and I have made sure the place never got robbed. I cannot leave until Tuesday. I have a flight at 10.00 a.m. I shall leave then!"

He thought about it for a few seconds and then said, "You can definitely leave by Tuesday?"

I said, "Yes, plus I will leave the key in the letter box for you."

He then said, "That's fine," and left.

My friend and I laughed for ages when he left. My friend said, "You told him."

I worked my nuts of every day, all weekend, and Monday until 10.00 p.m., when I reached the office, hoping and praying I had earned enough. I wouldn't have been happy if I didn't.

The tins we had for collecting money were larger than pint glasses, slightly taller, and nearly twice as wide, so held some serious coinage.

I put the money into the counting machine. This I had done many times, not just for myself but also for others. I was good friends with all staff and was a trustworthy part of the team. I would help out in the office many times.

Whilst I was pouring in the money from the first container, I was praying there would be enough. Both Geoffrey and Plugga were there to see this through.

I started to pour the second tin in, still praying. And fair play to the boys, they were being very supportive of me the whole time. They believed I had made enough, as the previous week's total had come to a huge amount. But I still needed to cover the many hundreds of Aussie dollars in wages to cover the debt, which was possible.

A big day at the races would do it, but I was just around town doing what I could. Nerves were getting the better of me as the third tin was going in. For me to have enough money, there needed to be enough to go up to the next banding of payment. The more I collecting the different pay percentages there were. So on the fourth nearly full tin, it was do or die, so to speak.

As the money spewed out of the tin, I could see more one-dollar and two-dollar coins coming out. I was feeling a little more relieved, as there could have been five-cent and ten-cent coins. As the dollars rolled out, it was looking good. Then the machine jammed, at just the critical point, making my nerves even more tethered.

I unjammed the machine and carried on with the counting. It came down to the wire. If the last few remaining coins came out as dollars, it would be done. If not, I was short. The coins came out of the tin and crashed into the counter. At first I couldn't see what they all were, as they went under the other coins. So we had to wait until the machine finished turning to see the final outcome. All I could hear was the sound of coins clanging and clashing. All three of us stood anxiously over the machine, waiting to see if I would make good on my promise.

The cogs turned. The money dropped. Did I make it or not? That was the question.

I totalled all the monies up ...and ...I was over by a few dollars and change.

Boom. With a leap in the air, I looked over to Geoffrey and Plugga. I saw they were just as ecstatic as I was. *Boom.* I was so happy that I'd worked as hard as I had and had given back every cent I'd borrowed.

Just before I left to go home and pack my bags (and also have a well-deserved sleep before my flight the next day), Plugga said, "Wait a minute. I have something for you."

I was like, *What can you have?*

He pulled an open tin off the shelves in the office and poured what was inside on the desk.

All I could see was what I hadn't seen for months—British currency. There were plenty of coins, pounds, and pence.

That was my parting gift from Plugga and the guys at the office. I counted it up, and it came to over thirty pounds. I was well happy. That was enough money to pay for my coach from Gatwick back to Cardiff. *Boom.* I thanked the guys profusely and went home.

The next day, they both came to the house as I was saying goodbye to my flatmate. We'd had some great times working and partying together, but now it was time for us both to move and part ways. He was still laughing as I left that he was renting a room off me whilst we were there squatting for free. He was a good lad.

At the airport, we promised we would stay in touch. I told them I would be back. And I did return a year or so later. We man hugged, and I left for my plane.

I was very sad to leave, but everything happens for a reason. No contact from my dad and no offer of help the whole time.

Thirty-two hours later, I arrived in Gatwick and headed towards the coach depot National Express to purchase my ticket to Cardiff, hoping it was still around or under thirty pounds. After asking at the counter, I knew I fortunately had enough. So I took out all the coins I had and passed them to the cashier. She then looked at me with a strange expression and said, "These fifty-pence pieces went out of circulation months ago."

I looked at her strange, as I had no idea. That was all the money I had, and it was mostly fifty-pence pieces.

I phoned a few friends to see if they would pick me up—to no avail.

I went to the chapel in Gatwick and prayed for some help. It came in the form of a priest. He asked, "How can I help you?"

I explained my dilemma, he asked to buy two fifty-pence pieces for a pound coin. Of course I obliged. He then asked, "Please wait here."

He left. I had nowhere to go, so I stayed.

He then returned a few minutes later and asked, "How many fifty-pence pieces do you have?"

I told him, and he bought them all for pound coins.

I asked, "Why would you buy them?"

He said, "I can use them in the phone box."

I made the transaction, thanked him, and left.

I paid for my coach ticket and headed for Cardiff, not knowing where I was going to go when I got there. I just relaxed, settled back for the three-hour coach ride, and enjoyed the scenery.

At Cardiff Central station, I got off the bus, picked up my suitcase from the luggage compartment, and wondered where to go from here. It was another point in my life where I wished I had someone who loved me.

At that point, I thought of my nan. I called her and explained my situation. And fair play, she said, "Come straight here."

I nearly cried at that point; it was unusual for someone to be nice, including family. But my nan had always been good to me. She was the only one.

So with my last remaining pennies, I bought a bus ticket to Caerphilly and walked the last few miles from Caerphilly to Llanbradach to a very nice welcome from my nan. Even my gramps made an effort to be welcoming. Much love Nan for always being there for me.

Before I move on, I would just like to add that, for the last few months, I have unwittingly and just by chance looked at either my phone, my computer clock, or another clock and seen 11:11. Most often, it was in the morning. But this also happened at night sometimes. I have been perplexed by this for a while now.

After hearing a friend randomly mention on Facebook they had been doing the same, it peaked my interest. I googled 11:11 and Google threw back 25,270,000 results. I was blown away. I read many of the results and will copy and paste one I found very interesting for you all to have a read. Here's what Uri Geller has to say about 11:11:

> I believe that people who have constant contact with the 1111 phenomena have some type of a positive mission to accomplish. It is still a mystery to me what it is that we all have to do or why we are all being gathered and connected together, but it is very real and tangible. I feel that it is immensely positive, almost like there is a thinking entity sending us these physical and visual signs from the universe. In me, it activates the power of prayer, love and determination to somehow help the world. Some day I suspect we will find out the true meaning behind this puzzling phenomenon.
>
> Blessings to you always

The 11:11 Awakening Code

There are many other very interesting explanations online of the 11:11 phenomenon.

A lot of people ask me, "Are you religious?"

I say, "No. I have a faith."

Then they ask, "Are you a Muslim?" Well, I especially get that question in West Africa.

My answer would be, "No. I'm universal". I believe that there is a divine creator who created this beautiful planet. I also believe that all religions have some good qualities.

As years ago, people or prophets never had temples, churches, or mosques to go and pray in, we can pray anywhere, and God will hear us.

Why go to a building and do it there, where, in most cases, you have a requirement to pay? Even if it is only a small amount of money, pay to pray is a ridiculous concept. Plus all prophets condoned peace and wanted all to be peaceful to others."

There are many mainstream media news outlets condemning Muslims as extremists, terrorists, or both. Don't get me wrong. There is and probably will always be a small number of religious fanatics or splinter cells around the globe. But there are nowhere near as many as the mainstream media reports to us. There are six corporations that run 99.9 per cent of the world news, so it's very easy to control with propaganda.

If you ever speak to a real Muslim, then you will know that Muslims are very loving, open, and caring.

I personally have great friends who are Muslims. I try not to put on any news channel, given my research into why it so detrimental to our well-being and our minds. TV takes us from a beta wave frame of mind to an alpha wave, which makes us believe and accept what we are being told, rather than questioning or examining the facts for ourselves.

Law of biogenesis and Noah's ark found on mount Ararat, extreme east of Turkey — I find both to be fascinating and I recommend worth studying.

Scientists have interlinked science with spiritualism and have discovered that, entangled in our DNA, all humans who've ever lived and are living now have an encoded message.

The encoded message reads ....God eternal within us.

Who do you know who questions anything anymore?

If everyone just took a minute, stepped back, and questioned the media, we would have truer answers, I would like to believe.

The truth will set you free.

Knowledge is power.

We all have the ability to read, learn, question everything, and think. Thinking is being, so please, let's all do more thinking before thinking becomes illegal.

Always think positively though. As scientists have proved, our minds are so powerful we control and create our reality by thought, words, and actions. In addition, thinking negatively has such a damning effect on us. Just a bad thought or word about yourself can cascade into a torrent of negativity; depression; and, in the worst circumstance, suicide. Right—less of the negativity and back to positivity.

We humans love a good heart-warming story. Well, at least the majority do. And we would like for the world to be, among many things, peaceful, with of course, no wars, starvation, homelessness, or diseases. And very importantly, we would like for everyone to be happy, healthy, and content.

We can do this quite easily. Let's take all the money for wars and put them towards clothing, feeding, housing, and educating everyone, ensuring that we do not leave anyone one out. This can be accomplished many times over. Please, I ask all to view on Youtube a video entitled *Bill Hicks, It's just a Ride.*
I would also recommend a documentary on you tube called…
"The Arrivals" all 52 parts. Very interesting and also very informative.

Now let's turn to diseases. All we need is for our doctors to stop prescribing to patients drugs that in most cases clearly don't work. We also need them to stop offering treatments that are detrimental to the patients' health through side effects. Let's make the big pharmaceutical corporations prove that they have cures for all diseases. Many people keep running around parks and donating to charities. For example, Cancer research is making billions of dollars. All the time, they will never admit to a cure. These evil tyrants don't care about us at all, at all, at all. Anybody can find this out with a modicum of research. Dr Otto Warburg first found a cure in the early 1900s. Plus, he won a Nobel Peace Prize for it. Many doctors since have found cures. Plus Canada has admitted they have a cure. Good one Canada.
The downside is that, if anyone or any company decided to come clean about having a cure for cancer, the government would have them arrested and tried in court.
"Why?" I hear you say.

It's because of the Cancer Act 1939. Cancer is a billion-dollar-a-year business. The greed of some people is too great for truth to be known.

GlaxoSmithKline, one of the, or the, largest pharmaceutical company on earth has just been sued for eight billion dollars. You never get sued for that much if your company is squeaky clean.

Happy, healthy and content—this covers a whole range of things, as everyone wants and desires different things. So let's keep it simple. Most people would like not to worry about money or even paying their bills—luxury off-grid living, I would say. But that's not for everyone. First things first; let's just have a bank in the country that's not owned by the Rothschild dynasty, so we can have a debt-free currency. Iceland and Saudi Arabia, just to name two, are countries with a no-debt currency. Then if your country is not at war, no taxes need to be paid. Thus, the money that is printed from your own country's bank pays for schools, hospitals, infrastructure, fire and police stations, as well as staff. "Sound ridiculous," I hear you say.

Not at all. A century ago America did just that.

That was before the oligarchy started sending troops to fight wars so the government could make money off the debt and steal resources from whatever country the fighting took place in. Sad but true.

From time to time I ask myself, *Am I a spiritual man?* Although not openly, so when I chat with people normally, sometimes I think that, with all the travelling I've done, the different countries and cultures I have submerged myself in, and the knowledge I have picked up along my journey of life, I believe I am. In a wondrous way, I feel enlightened and can hold a good argument to sustain my spiritual belief. This was not so much the case during my early years living in Wales, but after that I was travelling and living for a few months in Israel. I then went on to enjoy spending time with good honest Christians I met at work. Subsequently, I went to church with them and was baptised in Melbourne, Australia.

As a Christian, I never really went to church regularly after I returned to the United Kingdom, as it is a very satanically run country. I'm glad to be away from it. Primarily, it was my travels, which I breezed over in this book, along with living in West Africa that played a big part of my spiritual awakening to the materialistic world. I believe that I have subconsciously known this since I was a youngster, as I believe the calling to be spiritual is just to be good to yourself and others. Helping others in a good, honest, and caring way, is the highest calling. All prophets, regardless of religion, promoted the same, as I recall from knowledge and books I have read, with a range of subjects from Christianity to the Quran.

Reading about the Quran is very interesting and makes perfect sense. A lot of westerners would probably think I am crazy, not just because of what I have written. Even just to talk about reading something related to the Quran would send shivers down the spines of many westerners. However, those who read anything to do with Islam will soon see that it is a very peaceful and a very well-educated religion.

I would really like to help all who deserve and need help. This is why I am and will be putting serious effort into opening a clinic here in The Gambia; the President His Excellency Sheikh Professor Alhagi Dr Yahya AJJ Jammeh is well aware of the corruption around the world that I have been writing about and has condoned natural healing and the growing of one's own crops. In many countries, such things are illegal. He is a forward thinker and a great president in terms of keeping the country safe. Natural healing clinics are made possible here. My good friend Kyle Omailon is running an NGO here doing exactly this. He is saving lives on a daily basis, working seven days a week. The medicine and testimonies are here, and I can bear witness to some great healing myself. I definitely wouldn't offer the medicine if it wasn't beneficial. Even the board of health here scrutinises the naturopathy clinic.

My other plan to help the needy is to start up a charity online called Humanity Rules. The motto will read, "It's not just for one cause; it's for them all."   ·

Africa has beaten me, torn my insides out, and left me to dry.
Thats how I felt about Africa for a while.
But like I mentioned earlier it has ways of drawing you in to love it deeply.

Time has moved on its 28/02/18 and life is different here in The Gambia.

We have a new president, only time will tell if he can do a better job that the last dictator. I unfortunately know he won't but still like to believe that not all power players are heartless, money hungry despots.

I had returned to the UK for a year and a half and noticed big changes and can envision many more changes that were and are not to my liking.

Maybe the world has or hasn't changed, but I know one thing for sure— I have changed and changed for the better. I'm not an alcoholic or womaniser any longer, I have grown and matured even more than I was — still not to my full potential, but soon, very soon. Laus Deo.

Life truly has so many ups and downs, all to test our character.

I Urge you to study anything you didn't understand or even email me and I'll do my best to get back to you.

I have returned to The Gambia, West Africa and have opened a Clinic in Tanji. I will have been back a year in 7 days. I've settled in nicely made good friends and my patients respect me.

Life is good, quiet and easy.

So my plan from here ....

Is this..............

***

To be continued in my next book.

***

"Humanity Rules Foundation".
Any donations to help poor Africans would be appreciated.TIA.

Contact details are as follows:
+447492888333 WhatsApp
+2207565450
peacefulfreeman@yahoo.com
happymanclinic@yahoo.com

***

RIP Mybrid
RIP Kaddie
RIP Pako
RIP Simon Fenton
RIP Nan

It matters not who you love,
Where you love,
Why you love or how you love,
It matters only that you love.
—John Lennon, legend

Much love to you all. God speed.

Printed in the United States
By Bookmasters